GLOBALIZATION, GLOBALISM, ENVIRONMENTS, AND ENVIRONMENTALISM

Globalization, Globalism, Environments, and Environmentalism

Consciousness of Connections

The Linacre Lectures 2000

Edited by
STEVEN VERTOVEC
and
DARRELL POSEY

OXFORD
UNIVERSITY PRESS

OXFORD

UNIVERSITY PRESS

Great Clarendon Street, Oxford OX2 6DP

Oxford University Press is a department of the University of Oxford.
It furthers the University's objective of excellence in research, scholarship,
and education by publishing worldwide in

Oxford New York

Auckland Bangkok Buenos Aires Cape Town Chennai
Dar es Salaam Delhi Hong Kong Istanbul Karachi Kolkata
Kuala Lumpur Madrid Melbourne Mexico City Mumbai Nairobi
São Paulo Shanghai Singapore Taipei Tokyo Toronto

Oxford is a registered trade mark of Oxford University Press
in the UK and in certain other countries

Published in the United States
by Oxford University Press Inc., New York

British Library Cataloguing in Publication Data

Data available

Library of Congress Cataloging in Publication Data
Globalization, globalism, environment, and environmentalism: consciousness of
connections / edited by Steven Vertovec and Darrell Posey.
p. cm.—(Linacre lectures ; 2000)
Includes bibliographical references and index.
1. Environmental economics. 2. Globalization—Economic aspects.
3. Globalization—Environmental aspects. 4. Globalization—Social aspects.
5. Sustainable development—Citizen participation. 6. International economic
relations. I. Vertovec, Steven. II. Posey, Darrell Addison, 1947–
III. Linacre lectures ; 2000.
2003 333.7—dc22 2003060966
ISBN 0–19–926452–x

1 3 5 7 9 10 8 6 4 2

Typeset in Stempel Garamond
by Regent Typesetting, London
Printed in Great Britain
on acid-free paper by
Biddles Ltd,
Guildford and King's Lynn

ACKNOWLEDGEMENTS

This volume arises from the Linacre Lectures 2000, which was co-sponsored by the Transnational Communities Research Programme of the Economic and Social Research Council (UK). Much of the inspiration and organization of the series came from Darrell Posey, whose death in 2001 came as a great loss to many friends and colleagues across the world. This volume is dedicated to the work and spirit of Darrell Posey.

I wish to thank Oxford colleagues who play key roles in developing the seminar series and book, especially Paul Slack and Jane Edwards at Linacre College, Oxford, and Anna Winton and Emma Newcombe of the Transnational Communities Programme. I would also like to thank Kristina Plenderleith for her help in compiling a bibliography for Darrell Posey's chapter. This book was completed while I was a Fellow at the Wissenschaftskolleg/Institute for Advanced Study, Berlin, to which I am very grateful for its superb services.

Steven Vertovec
Berlin, October 2002

CONTENTS

CONTRIBUTORS

Manuel Castells, Professor of Sociology and Professor of City and Regional Planning, University of California, Berkeley.

Herbert Girardet, Chairman of the Schumacher Society and an Associate Editor of *Resurgence*.

Calestous Juma, Director of the Science, Technology and Innovation Program at the Center for International Development, Harvard University.

Marcia Langton, Professor (Foundation Chair) of Indigenous Studies, Melbourne University.

Lord Peter Melchett, former executive director of Greenpeace UK, now consultant with Burson-Marsteller.

Eugene Odum (*d.* 2002) was Director Emeritus of the University of Georgia Institute of Ecology. He is recognized world-wide as 'the father of modern ecology'.

Darrell Posey (*d.* 2001) was an anthropologist and ethnobiologist, well known for his research on Amazonia and a Fellow of Linacre College, Oxford.

Chris Rose, former Deputy Director of Greenpeace.

Maurice Strong, Chairman of the Earth Council in Canada.

Steven Vertovec, Professor of Transnational Anthropology, University of Oxford, and Senior Research Fellow at Linacre College, Oxford.

Steven Yearley is Professor and Head of Department of Sociology, University of York.

ABBREVIATIONS

BSE	bovine spongiform encephalopathy
BTU	British thermal unit
CBD	Convention on Biological Diversity
CHP	combined heat and power
CITES	Convention on International Trade in Endangered Species (of Wild Flora and Fauna)
COICA	Co-ordinating Group of the Indigenous Peoples of the Amazon Basin
CPRE	Council for the Protection of Rural England
CTE	Committee on Trade and Environment
ECF	elemental chlorine-free
FSC	Forest Stewardship Council
GATT	General Agreement on Tariffs and Trade
GCC	Global Climate Coalition
GEF	Global Environment Facility
GM	genetically modified
GNP	gross national product
ICAO	International Civil Aviation Organization
ICOMOS	International Council on Monuments and Sites
IMF	International Monetary Fund
IPCC	Intergovernmental Panel on Climate Change
IPR	intellectual properly rights
LBG	lesbian, bisexual, gay
MEA	Multilateral Environmental Agreement
MFN	most favoured nation
MSC	Marine Stewardship Council
NGO	non-governmental organization
NIMBY	not-in-my-back-yard
POPs	persistent organic pollutants
PPM	processes and production method
pv	photovoltaic
SMO	social movement organization
TCF	totally chlorine-free
TRIPS	trade-related aspects of intellectual properties
UN	United Nations

UNCED	United National Conference on Environment and Development
UNDP	UN Development Programme
UNESCO	UN Educational, Scientific and Cultural Organization
UNEP	UN Environment Programme
WMO	World Meteorological Office
WTO	World Trade Organization
WWF	Worldwide Fund for Nature

Introduction

Steven Vertovec

SCIENTISTS, politicians, businesspeople and the wider public today have an increasing awareness of global environmental issues. This public awareness, and a certain amount of knowledge accompanying it, has been growing in depth and breadth. Such an awareness has been developing over decades, spurred by prominent publications such as Rachel Carson's (1963) *Silent Spring*, the Club of Rome's (1972) *The Limits of Growth*, and the Brundtland Commission's (1987) *Our Common Future*. Major public events have also drawn world-wide attention to environmental matters, especially the 1972 UN Conference on the Human Environment organized in Stockholm, the 1992 UN Conference on Environment and Development (UNCED, often known as the Earth Summit) in Rio de Janeiro, and most recently the 2002 World Summit on Sustainable Development held in Johannesburg.

Global environmental problems were regarded as minor issues marginal to national interests until the 1980s. It was in the middle of the 1980s that the mass media began to pay increased attention to global environmental issues, prompted by events such as the Bhopal and Chernobyl disasters and the discovery of a hole in the ozone layer over the Antarctic. Since then, there has been a rising interest in such problems, particularly in the light of issues of global warming, along with unease over the emission of toxic chemicals, threats to biodiversity, desertification, the depletion of the world's fisheries and the elimination of forest cover. There has emerged especially since that decade a world-wide attentiveness to common risks posed by radioactivity, pollutants and depletion of resources (cf. Beck 1992). Over the past twenty years, not least urged by public concern, scientific understanding of the global environment has developed considerably, occasionally feeding into public awareness. William C. Clark (2000: 87) describes the development of scientific awareness of global connections among environmental 'stuff': 'As understanding of the earth system has emerged during the last two decades, it has revealed the planet's environment to be shaped by complex linkages among atmosphere, ocean, soil and biota.'

Since the 1980s a rising environmental consciousness has become manifest in a variety of ways (cf. Viola 1998). These include:

- an exponential rise in the number of environment-focused grassroot and non-government organizations (part of the massive growth of international NGOs, from some 13,000 in 1981 to over 47,000 in 2001; Anheier and Themudo 2002). Margaret E. Keck and Kathryn Sikkink (1998: 128) point to how major environmental organizations in the latter half of the 1980s, equipped with computers for direct mail techniques for fundraising and membership management, grew rapidly: 'Total membership of ten organizations for which continuous data are available grew from 4,198,000 in 1976 to 5,816,000 in 1986 and 8,270,000 in 1990';
- a proliferation of official environmental agencies at national levels (from two such agencies world-wide in 1970 to over 180 by 1995);
- the setting up of intergovernmental organizations and agreements, including the United Nations Environmental Programme, the Vienna Convention and the Kyoto Protocol;
- the creation of numerous environmental science institutions, committees, international conferences and university courses;
- the growth of 'green' consumerism as seen in the popularity of organically grown foods, 'fair-trade' products, recycled and recyclable materials, energy-efficient appliances and raw materials sustainably produced.

In these ways a global 'consciousness of connections' is taking concrete form. This volume presents the views of a number of leading figures surrounding the nature of such consciousness and the nature of different kinds of global connections within and between the realms of: globalization (including the process of creating or intensifying social, political and economic networks), globalism (our sense of the world as a whole), specific environments (such as cities), and environmentalism (expressed in the activities of social movement organizations).

The notion of 'globalism' is central to an understanding of what is meant in this volume by 'consciousness of connections'. Globalism refers to an appreciation of the world as a single place or space (cf. Robertson 1992) and the ways in which people have internalized a basic view of the world as a common domain in which activities or events (natural or man-made) in one part might have profound effects in another, distant one. It is an awareness of large-scale knock-on effects. Maurice Strong points out in his contribution to this volume that the environmental movement as a whole has at its core such a consciousness of complex relationships linking local conditions across the planet. These days people are not surprised to hear about, for instance, how the pollution associated with an industrial accident somewhere can have devastating consequences on ecosystems or human health in places far away. As Robert O. Keohane and Joseph S. Nye (2002: 9) put it, 'The environmental motto "everything is connected to everything else" warns us that there may be unanticipated effects of many human activities, from burning carbon fuels (generating climate change) to genetically modifying crops grown for food.'

The connections within environmental systems—including humans and their activities—are known be symbiotic. 'The stage' and 'the actors'—as one of the founding figures of ecology, Eugene Odum (in this volume) reminds us—are constantly interacting. When approaching a variety of economic, political and environmental issues it is increasingly urgent to adopt an ecological or ecosystems approach which inherently recognizes forms of interconnectedness. In their chapters Odum and Juma highlight core ecological principles for such an approach, especially regarding diversity, disequilibrium and irreversibility. These concepts have become central to numerous scientific, technical and political agendas. Ecological connectedness is inherent in the world-views and spirituality of many indigenous peoples, described in this volume by Darrell Posey and Marcia Langton (also see Posey 1999). Chris Rose and Peter Melchett underscore the need to use holistic ecosystems thinking to 'design-out problems' when tackling these issues. And Herbert Girardet describes how an eco-systems approach is valuable to understanding the growth and dynamics of cities.

Another mode of connection concerns the ways that the environment has become central to discussion of foreign and domestic political economy. 'These issues are no longer viewed as merely scientific and technical issues,' write Gareth Porter *et al.* (2000: 1), 'but as intertwined with central issues in world politics: the international system of resource production and use, the liberalization of world trade, North–South relations, and even international conflict and internal social and political stability.' One key notion linking these domains, as Calestous Juma recounts in this volume, is that of sustainability—a concept first prominently put to the fore in the Brundtland Commission's (1987) *Our Common Future*. While economists and ecologists have long held diametrically opposed views on development, the view emphasized by the Brundtland Commission was that development and the environment are inextricably linked. 'That compromise generated a good deal of euphoria. Green groups grew concerned over poverty, and development charities waxed lyrical about greenery' (*The Economist* 2002: 4). In our present terminology, we can say that the idea of sustainability allows for a significant consciousness of connections between economic and environmental issues. Despite its shortcomings, according to John Graham (ibid.) the notion of sustainability 'forces integrated policy-making. In practical terms, it means that you have to take economic cost-benefit trade-offs into account in environmental laws, and keep environmental trade-offs in mind with economic development.'

It has become an accepted state of affairs that environmental problems and threats cannot be dealt with by policies of individual states (see, for instance, Grundmann 2001). The spread of environment-focused ideas and strategies (such as sustainable development) now regularly underpin and enhance information transfer and the shaping of policy between governments. This has been noticed in the activities of inter-governmental bodies. 'It is abundantly clear,' Clark (2000: 99) says, 'that the networks of connections running through inter-government organizations dealing with environmental issues have thickened appreciably during the past several decades.'

Inter-governmental activities represent one facet of globalization, here understood as 'the widening, deepening and speeding up of worldwide interconnectedness in all aspects of contemporary social life' (Held et al. 1999: 2). More popular understandings focus only on economic aspects, conceived as growing economic interdependence through cross-border transactions of goods, services and finance. Liberalization and the reduction of barriers to the flow of trade and investment are often seen as the instruments of this kind of globalization. As Rose and Melchett argue, the view that economic globalization threatens the environment is clichéd. It is certainly true that intensified global economic activities lead to an increasing consumption of fossil fuels, a rising volume of hazardous and other wastes, concentration of populations in mega-cities, and disastrous levels of exploitation of natural resources such as forests, fisheries and freshwater. However, other modes of globalization have the potential to promote a more efficient and less environmentally damaging set of social and economic transformations (see, respectively, Strong and Castells, this volume). These include shifting production from raw materials-based manufacturing to knowledge-based industries, and using clean technologies to reduce pollution (Chung and Gillespie 1998).

With reference to globalization as interconnectedness, the notion of 'consciousness of connections' has yet another meaning. This relates to the growth in the number of links between a range of individuals, groups and organizations concerned with environmental issues around the world. Here, Maurice Strong suggests that globalization has been a 'mixed blessing' for environmentalists: while the intensification of global economic activity has contributed significantly to environmental deterioration, globalization as the extension of a global civil society through organizational networking has facilitated increased public awareness of environmental issues around the world. Similarly, in this volume Manuel Castells describes how a global network of interaction linking metropolitan nodes can bring mutual benefit as well as ecological crisis.

In their respective chapters, Steven Yearley and Maurice Strong both point to the 1992 Earth Summit as a key event which transformed the nature of activities and connections between environmental movements. Since then we have witnessed the creation of several world-wide environmental advocacy coalitions. '[T]hey involve networks cutting across not only actors but also scales. The result is globe-spanning networks of knowledge and practices, connected to multiple local action coalitions that are individually attuned to the politics and ecology of particular places' (Clark 2000: 101). Indeed, as Robin Cohen and Shirin Rai (2000: 9) suggest, 'without transnational co-ordination environmental movements simply are impotent'. The Internet has been invaluable to such networking, of course, as evidenced by such sites as www.interconnection.org, which serve to develop and link NGOs worldwide and especially in developing countries.

Connections between environmental groups are expanding in many directions. The consciousness of connections between environmental and other issues has led to the gradual decline of single-issue activism. There are now growing links between environmental groups and anti-globalization/anti-capitalist movements. In summarizing the (limited) results of the 2002 Johannesburg summit on sustainable development, *The Economist* (2002: 14) felt that the event 'marked a shift in the role that agencies other than governments—be they green groups, charities aiming to relieve poverty, or big business—can play. Dozens of new partnerships were launched to tackle specific local problems, and hundreds of existing ones were examined and discussed. This marketplace of ideas and experiments is the nitty-gritty of sustainable development.' While what are called 'type 1' partnerships refer to government-to-government relations, the Johannesburg summit highlighted the spread of 'type 2' partnerships, which are between governments, businesses, NGOs and local community groups (ibid.). Robin Cohen and Paul Kennedy (2000: 338) see the new flexibility of environmental groups and their networks as a strength:

Because global problems demand global solutions it is hardly surprising that the green movement has increasingly sought to operate transnationally. Partly, what enables green groups to be globally effective is their capacity to construct viable linkages between different countries, groups and issues. But what also empowers them is their growing ability to collaborate with powerful elite interests when that appears useful while activating transnational grassroots support for more radical agendas whenever the opposition to change displayed by the former makes this necessary.

Clark (2000: 101–2) proposes that 'If we choose to make the qualifying condition for "environmental globalism" the existence of a rich network of environmentally mediated linkages among actors at multicontinental distance, then environmental globalism is unequivocally a salient feature of modern society.' How such environmental globalism, or consciousness of connections, becomes further manifest remains to be seen. The desirability of drawing upon such globalism to construct structures for global governance continues to be contested (cf. Juma and Strong in this volume). In any case, today's critical problems of environmental pollution, exploitation and deterioration require the political will to do something about them. The growing awareness of environmental issues and connections, and the networks arising around them, will hopefully serve to catalyse and support such a will world-wide.

REFERENCES

Anheier, Helmut and Nuno Themudo (2002). 'Organizational forms of global civil society: implications of going global', in M. Glasius, M. Kaldor and H. Anheier (eds.), *Global Civil Society 2002*. Oxford: Oxford University Press, 191–216.

Beck, Ulrich (1992) *Risk Society: Toward a New Modernity*. London: Sage.

Brundtland, Gro Harlem/World Commission on Environment and Development (1987). *Our Common Future*. Oxford: Oxford University Press.

Carson, Rachel (1963). *Silent Spring*. London: Hamish Hamilton.

Chung, Chris and Brendan Gillespie (1998). 'Globalization and the environment: new challenges for the public and private sectors', in *Globalization and the Environment: Perspectives from OECD and Dynamic Non-Member Economies*. Paris: Organization for Economic Co-operation and Development, 7–15.

Clark, William C. (2000) 'Environmental globalism,' in J. S. Nye and J. D. Donahue (eds.), *Governance in a Globalizing World*. Washington, DC.: Brookings Institution Press, 86–108.

Club of Rome (1972). *The Limits of Growth: A Report for the Club of Rome's Project on the Predicament of Mankind*. London: Earth Island

Cohen, Robin and Paul Kennedy (2000). *Global Sociology*. Basingstoke: Macmillan.

Cohen, Robin and Shirin Rai (2000). 'Introduction', in R. Cohen and S. Rai (eds.), London: *Global Social Movements*. Athlone, 1–17.

The Economist (2002). 'How many planets? A survey of the global environment'. 6 July 2002.

Grundmann, Reiner (2001). *Transnational Environmental Policy: Reconstructing Ozone*. London: Routledge.

Held, D., A. McGrew, D. Goldblatt and J. Perraton (1999). *Global Transformations: Politics, Economics, Culture*. Cambridge: Polity.

Keck, Margaret E. and Kathryn Sikkink (1998). *Activists beyond Borders: Advocacy Networks in International Politics*. Ithaca: Cornell University Press.

Keohane, Robert O. and Joseph S. Nye (2000). 'Introduction', in J. S. Nye and J. D. Donahue (eds.), *Governance in a Globalizing World*. Washington, DC: Brookings Institution Press, 1–41.

Porter, Gareth, Janet Welsh Brown and Pamela S. Chasek (2000). *Global Environmental Politics*, 3rd edn. Boulder, CO: Westview Press.

Posey, Darrell Addison (ed.) (1999). *Cultural and Spiritual Values of Biodiversity*. London: Intermediate Technology for the UN Environmental Development Programme.

Robertson, Roland (1992). *Globalization: Social Theory and Global Culture*. London: Sage.

Viola, Eduardo (1998). 'Globalization, environmentalism and new transnational social forces,' in *Globalization and the Environment: Perspectives from OECD and Dynamic Non-Member Economies*, Paris: Organization for Economic Co-operation and Development, 39–52.

How Ecology Has Changed

Eugene P. Odum

DURING the past half century, ecology has emerged from its roots in biology to become a stand-alone discipline that interfaces organisms, the physical environment and human affairs. This is in line with the root meaning of the word ecology which is 'the study of the household' or the total environment in which we live.

When I first came to the University of Georgia in 1940 as an instructor in the Department of Zoology, ecology was considered a rather unimportant sub-division of biology. At the end of World War II, we had a staff meeting to discuss 'core curriculum', or what courses every biology major should be required to take. My suggestion that ecology should be part of this core was rejected by all other members of the staff; they said ecology was just descriptive natural history with no basic principles. It was this 'put down', as it were, that started me thinking about a textbook that would emphasize basic principles, which eventually became the first edition of my *Fundamentals of Ecology*, published in 1953.

In those early days 'ecology' was often defined as the 'study of organisms in relation to environment'. The environment was considered a sort of inert stage in which the actors, that is the organisms, played the game of natural selection. Now we recognize that the 'stage' and the 'actors' interact with each other constantly so that not only do organisms relate to the physical environment, but they also change the environment. Thus, when the first green microbes, the *cynobacteria*, began putting oxygen into the atmosphere, the environment was greatly changed, making way for a whole new set of aerobic organisms.

Also, when one goes from the study of structure to the study of function, then the physical sciences (including energetics, biogeochemical cycling and earth sciences in general) have to be included. And, of course, now more than ever, we have to consider humans and the social sciences as part of the environment. So we now have essentially a new discipline of 'ecology' that is a three-way interface.

HIERARCHICAL ORGANIZATION

Since the affairs of both humans and nature tend to be hierarchically organized, we can review the changes of emphasis in ecology in terms of two very basic hierarchies: the levels of organization hierarchy and the energetic hierarchy.

Some contingent functions such as energetics operate the same at all levels, that is, the laws of thermodynamics apply to all levels, but other functions such as cybernetics operate differently at different levels. In systems language we can say that some systems behaviour changes with scale, or large is different from small.

Controls are 'set point' at all levels of the organism and below. Genes, hormones and nerve centres control growth and size within very narrow limits. Thus, when one's liver reaches the optimum size, it stops growing in size but will continue to improve in function. Any further growth in size is cancer and deadly. This very tight cybernetics is called 'homeostasis'. In sharp contrast, there are no 'set point' controls at the population, ecosystem or ecosphere levels, no thermostats, chemostats or 'demonstates' that control population size or the earth's climate. But there are negative feedbacks. When size overshoots some limit or carrying capacity, or a meteorological factor exceeds the current climatic mean, then downsizing or reversal occurs. Accordingly, balances in nature are not steady-state or equilibria, but are pulsing states. In my most recent textbook (Odum, 1997*a*) I suggest we use the term 'homeorheysis' (pulsing like a river) for this kind of control. (For more on the concept of the 'pulsing paradigm' see Odum, Odum, and Odum (1995).)

Since there is no set point at which the growth of human society goes from increasing returns of scale to decreasing returns of scale, or 'too much of good things', we are destined to overshoot the earth's life-support carrying capacity and to experience periods of downsizing, if quality of life is to be maintained. At present, the momentum in the growth of the human population is so great that it will double at least one more time—to maybe 12 billion—by 2050 (see Bongaart, 1994). This will hopefully be followed by a period of negative growth. In fact, some European countries are now at zero population growth as far as births and deaths are concerned, but are still growing due to immigration.

The energy hierarchy story is illustrated by the food chain and fossil fuel. As energy is transformed from one form to another the quantity decreases, but the concentration or quality of that which is transformed increases—a kind of bad news–good news story. I suspect that 90 per cent of people (including many ecologists) are completely unaware that different forms of energy are not the same in terms of work ability; one calorie or joule of sunlight is not the same as one calorie or joule of coal or oil. Sunlight will not run your car unless it is concentrated to a higher quality such as electricity. Thus, it takes some 10^5 calories of sunlight to make one calorie of predator and at least 2000 calories of sun to make one calorie of coal. Accordingly, running a city on solar power when the fossil fuels are used up is not going to be an easy or cheap transition. One reason for confusion about energy quantity and quality is that we have many terms for quantity (calories, joules, BTUs, horsepower and so on) but no widely used term for quality. My brother Howard has introduced the term 'emergy' to fill this language void. (For a brief review of this term and suggestions for using energy rather than money to valuate ecosystem services, see Odum and Odum, 2000.)

THE P/R RATIO AND MAINTENANCE AS THE ULTIMATE LIMITATION

The way we view ecological succession, or ecosystem development as I prefer to call it, has changed. The process is now best described in terms of community metabolism rather than, or in addition to, species composition. In successional stages P, or community gross production, exceeds R, or community respiration (= maintenance) with the mature or 'climax' stage developing when P = R or P/R = 1. Species composition is not a good indicator of climax because it varies greatly according to climate, topography and disturbance. The important principle regarding species composition is the shift from R-selection to K-selection. Opportunistic species with large families (producing numerous seeds or offspring) colonize the early stages, while survival of the individual is more important than the quantity of reproduction in the mature stages. There is, of course, an important parallel in the development of human society. In nature, very few species can make the R to K transition, so very few, if any, species are found in both pioneer and mature stages. Thus, surviving this transition is a major challenge for humans!

Another point to be made that has relevance in human affairs is that any system where R exceeds P (that is maintenance cost exceeds available resources) is not sustainable unless there are subsidies from outside (the source-sink concept). So, maintenance is the ultimate limitation for both humans and nature. And then there is the 'network law' that the cost of maintenance is a power function of size and complexity of the system. Thus, when a city or forest doubles in size the cost of maintenance more than doubles. When the city doubles, *per capita* taxes have to be increased to 'pump out the disorder' inherent in large, complex systems.

C. P. SNOW'S THIRD CULTURE

In 1959, English author and distinguished scientist Sir Charles P. Snow wrote a widely cited book entitled *The Two Cultures* in which he expressed concern about the lack of communication between the humanities and the sciences. In a second edition in 1963, he suggested that a 'third culture' would have to emerge to close this communication gap, which seemed to be getting wider as disciplines in both the sciences and the humanities were becoming more and more reductionist, fragmented and specialized. In contrast, ecology is a discipline that has in recent years been moving in the opposite direction, that is, increasing the scale of study to whole systems, landscapes and on up to the ecosphere. Accordingly, I have suggested that at these holistic levels, ecology is a candidate for Snow's third culture (Odum 1997*b*).

Edward Goldsmith, in his book *The Way: An Ecological World View* (1996 and 1998) argues at much length and with great intensity that what is needed is no less than a major paradigm shift from reductionist science and fragmented one-problem-one-solution technology to an ecological world-view that would provide a more holistic and long-term approach to dealing with our increasingly endangered earthly home. Since it is very unlikely that such a major paradigm shift will occur any time soon (at least, not until after the overshoot, as discussed earlier in this paper), I argue that in the mean time developing a third culture bridge is practicable—and a step in the right direction. What we are learning from nature about youth to maturity or quantitative to qualitative growth patterns, food chain energetics, feedback cybernetics, carrying capacity, evolution of competition to mutualism, diversity, networks and other ecosystem-level processes can help us build these culture bridges.

In summary, science and technology alone will not prevent global environmental deterioration because the problems and the solutions involve people and the non-science disciplines, especially economics, law, education, political science, and the social sciences.

HUMANITY'S TWO HOUSES AND THE CONCEPTS OF THE TECHNO-ECOSYSTEM AND REWARD FEEDBACK

Because of the tremendous difference between solar power and fossil fuel power, it may be helpful to think in terms of two environmental 'houses' rather than one, acting as a parasite–host system. Current urban-industrial society not only impacts upon natural ecosystems, but also creates entirely new arrangements called techno-ecosystems, a term that I believe was first suggested by landscape ecologist Zev Neveh (1982). These new systems utilize powerful energy sources (fossil and atomic fuels) and involve technology, money and cities which have few, if any, parallels in nature. If urban-industrial society is to survive in our finite world, it is important that techno-ecosystems interface with natural ecosystems in a more positive, mutualistic manner than is now the case.

Prior to the industrial revolution, humans were a part of, rather that apart from, nature. We were hunters and gatherer omnivores, acting as top predators in the food web. Early agricultural practices, like those still used in small family farms in the pre-industrial parts of the world, were compatible with natural ecosystems. Indeed, they often enriched the landscape in addition to providing food. The basic natural ecosystem model, however, is no longer adequate to take account of modern human activities that include: replacement of the less concentrated sunlight-based energy sources with fossil fuels; mushrooming growth of cities; rapidly expanding industrial agriculture and especially the increasing use of a money-based market economics as a basis for decision-making. Thus, we need to think and act in terms of new models that relate to two 'houses' as two interdependent systems.

Modern cities are major techno-ecosystems. They are very energetic hot spots requiring a very large area of low-energy density countryside to support it (the 'ecological footprint' concept). Current cities clean and recycle no air or water (to point of being potables), grow little or no food, recycle few basic nutrients, and generate huge amounts of waste that impact very large areas of downstream and downwind rural landscapes, rivers and oceans. Cities do export money to pay for natural resources converted into manufactured goods and services—but few are for non-market life-supporting goods and services of nature. Clean air and water, for example, are considered 'external' to the market and are 'free' to be consumed with little or no limitations. In other words, we pay people for services, but not ecosystems.

CONCLUSION

In summary, the two houses of humans operate too much like a parasite–host system. To call our modern civilization a parasite is not to belittle it, but to be realistic. Under natural selection in nature, parasites and hosts co-evolve for coexistence. Otherwise, if the parasite takes too much from the host, both die. This is especially the case where the parasite has only one host. Humans have only one host, since colonizing any other planet on any large scale is unlikely any time soon—if ever.

It is important that we increase the effort and money devoted to servicing our life-support ecosystems. I think most ecologists are not yet familiar with the concept of reward feedback. This refers to things that parasites,
predators and herbivores do to enhance the survival of their food supplies.
For example, when grazers such as grasshoppers, antelopes or cows eat
grass, their saliva contains growth hormones that stimulate the grass to put
up new shoots (see Dyer *et al.* 1993 and 1995). We desperately need to
increase the reward feedback flow from techno-ecosystems to natural
ecosystems. To accomplish reward feedback, we need to 'reconstruct' economics to include life-supporting goods and service (natural capital) as
suggested by economist Kenneth Boulding some 40 years ago (1962) and
now widely discussed by economists and ecologists. (See, for example, the
1999 book entitled *Natural Capitalism: Creating the Next Industrial
Revolution*, written by businessperson Paul Hawken and ecologists
Amory and Hunter Lovins.)

The creation of such modes of reward feedback would mark a profound
turning-point, reflecting how the rise of the study of ecology has affected
our world-view and how this, in turn, can impact upon the development of
our life-support ecosystems.

REFERENCES

Bongaart, J. (1994). 'Population policy options in the developing world',
    Science, 263: 771–6.
Boulding, K. (1962). *The Reconstruction of Economics*. New York: Science
    Editions.
Dyer, M. I., C. L. Turner, and T. R. Seastedt. (1993). 'Herbivory and its
    consequences', *Ecological Applications*, 3: 10–16.
Dyer, M. I., A. M. Moon, M. R. Brown, and D. A. Crossley, Jr (1995).
    'Grasshopper crop and midgut extract effect on plants: an example of
    reward feedback', *Proceedings of the National Academy of Sciences*, 92:
    5475–8.
Goldsmith, E. (1996). *The Way: An Ecological World View*. Devon, UK:
    Themis Books; revised edn 1998, Athens, GA: University of Georgia
    Press.
Hawken, P., A. Lovins and H. Lovins (1999). *Natural Capital: Creating
    the Next Industrial Revolution*. New York: Little, Brown.
Nevah, Z. (1982). 'Landscape ecology as an emerging branch of human
    ecosystem science', *Advances in Ecological Research*, 12: 189–237.
Odum, E. P. (1997a). *Ecology: A Bridge between Science and Society*.
    Sunderland, MA: Sinauer Associates.

Odum, E. P. (1997*b*). 'Can ecology contribute to C. P. Snow's third culture?' *Bulletin of the Ecological Society of America*, 78(3): 134.

Odum, H. T. and E. P. Odum (2000). 'The energetic basis for valuation of ecosystem services', *Ecosystems*, 3: 21–3.

Odum, W. E., E. P. Odum, and H. T. Odum (1995). 'Nature's pulsing paradigm', *Estuaries*, 18: 547–55.

Snow, C. P. (1963). *The Two Cultures: A Second Look*. New York: Cambridge University Press.

2

International Trade and Environment: Towards Integrative Responsibility

Calestous Juma

THE rise of environmental awareness and the advent of globalization have emerged as two of the most important forces shaping international trends in the new century (Taylor and Thomas 1999). Interest in environmental and trade issues is not new; however, the intensity with which these forces are considered to be in conflict with each other is new. These two forces represent two seemingly different stylized epistemological outlooks. On the one hand, international trade is driven by technological innovation and expressed as discrete and reducible entities such as products and prices. Environmental concerns, on the other hand, are linked to the growing understanding of the complex relationships between natural and cultural evolution.

As globalization continues to rise, growing efforts are under way to ensure that international trade be consistent with other societal goals, such as environmental conservation. Finding complementary goals for these two regimes has been challenging in the past (Repetto 1993). This is not just an academic exercise but a serious attempt to create international agreements on how to integrate environment and trade activities. The results of such efforts are codified in the Rio Declaration[1] and Chapter 2 of Agenda 21,[2] as well as reflected in a number of international environmental

---

[1] Principle 12 of the Rio Declaration states that: 'States should co-operate to promote a supportive and open international economic system that would lead to economic growth and sustainable development in all countries, to better address the problems of environmental degradation. Trade policy measures for environmental purposes should not constitute a means of arbitrary or unjustifiable discrimination or a disguised restriction on international trade. Unilateral actions to deal with environmental challenges outside the jurisdiction of the importing country should be avoided.'

[2] Chapter 2 of Agenda 21 states that: 'Environment and trade policies should be mutually supportive. An open, multilateral trading system makes possible a more efficient allocation and use of resources and thereby contributes to an increase in production and incomes and to lessening demands on the environment. It thus provides additional resources needed for

agreements dealing with toxic chemicals and genetically modified organisms. These treaties[3] contain provisions that seek to ensure that international trade and environmental protection are mutually supportive.

These agreements are also matched by efforts at the national level to integrate economic and environmental considerations. Such efforts received global legitimacy with the adoption of *Our Common Future*, the report of the Commission on Environment and Development released in 1987 under the chairmanship of Norwegian Prime Minister Gro Harlem Brundtland. The report advanced the principle of integrative responsibility, which became the basis for the work of the 1992 United Nations Conference on Environment and Development (UNCED). UNCED adopted Agenda 21—forging the most elaborate effort yet to provide guidelines for implementing integrative responsibility.

Also adopted were the Rio Principles on Environment and Development, which also articulate and push for integrative responsibility among these two factions. Indeed, Principle 16 of the Rio Declaration on Environment and Development states that national 'authorities should endeavour to promote the internalization of environmental costs and the use of economic instruments, taking into account the approach that the polluter should, in principle, bear the cost of pollution, with due regard to the public interest and without distorting international trade and investment.'

Although national efforts are important, they have not generated as much interest as global concerns. This chapter examines the relationships between international trade and environment and argues that the integration of the two will depend largely on the growth in ecological knowledge and reform in national and international institutions.

To elaborate this argument, the chapter is divided into three parts. The first part outlines the key trade and environment norms that guide the debate. The second section examines the relationship between ecology, technology and property rights. These sections show that although globalization and environmental management appear to be in conflict, approaches that recognize institutional diversity are likely to lead to greater integration between the two. The last section focuses on the importance of ecological knowledge and institutional innovation. As a whole,

---

economic growth and development and improved environmental protection. A sound environment, on the other hand, provides the ecological and other resources needed to sustain growth and underpin a continuing expansion of trade. An open, multilateral trading system, supported by the adoption of sound environmental policies, would have a positive impact on the environment and contribute to sustainable development.'

    [3] These are the Rotterdam Convention on the Prior Informed Consent, and the Cartagena Protocol on Biosafety to the Convention on Biological Diversity.

the chapter cautions against institutional determinism and stresses that new governance structures should co-evolve with the growth of ecological knowledge.

TRADE AND ENVIRONMENT NORMS

Normative standards

The relationship between trade and environment is one of the most controversial issues in international politics. This issue is an extension of domestic debates over the impact of economic activities on the environment. World-wide trends show growing environmental degradation that is directly linked to economic activities. National trends have been amplified to the global level through attempts to show that international trade is harmful to the environment (Xing and Kolstad 1998). In fact, the rise of the environmental movement was closely associated with concerns over industrial pollution and subsequent claims that polluting factories were being relocated from the industrialized countries to the developing nations (Eskeland and Harrison 1997).

The exact impact of international trade on the environment has been a matter of considerable debate since the late 1960s (GATT 1971), and the emergence of the globalization paradigm has added to the intensity of this debate. Many of the concerns expressed about the impact of international trade on the environment are genuine and deserve attention. There are numerous claims about these impacts, however, that are driven by wider socio-economic concerns. For example, those concerned about the impact of trade liberalization in agriculture have often cited environmental and other concerns as a basis for challenging globalization. Many of these socio-economic concerns are also linked to a drive to create regional markets as well as to preserve traditional trading patterns.

The absence of evidence on what impact international trade is having on the environment, however, will not prevent debate on the issue. This is largely because the normative standards guiding activities in both regimes differ in the degree of entrenchment and content. The trade regime is a discernible, though disputed, jurisprudence that is expressed in a wide range of institutions—the World Trade Organization (WTO) being the latest and most robust. Ecological jurisprudence, on the other hand, is relatively young, although many of its guiding principles, such as diversity, interconnectedness, irreversibility and time-dependence have been part of the human consciousness for millennia. Global environmental institutions are still in their early stages of development. As we will later see, debate on the development of these institutions is currently being driven by political rather than normative goals. It is notable that trade institutions are a product of a long history of experimentation. The idea of creating a world trade organization was first proposed in 1919 and realized in 1994. This long time frame is accounted for by the complexity of the regime.

The trade regime is constructed around the concept that non-discrimination is expressed through two fundamental principles: the most-favoured nation (MFN) principle and the national treatment principle. Under MFN, WTO members must accord to any product in international trade the same treatment to all other member states. This provision guarantees equal treatment for all member states. Under the principle of national treatment all imported products are treated in the same way as domestic products. In addition to these principles, there are measures that prohibit the use of quantitative restrictions that might favour domestic products.

Article XX of the General Agreement on Tariffs and Trade (GATT), however, grants exemptions to measures 'necessary to protect human, animal or plant life or health' or 'relating to the conservation of exhaustible natural resources if such measures are made effective in conjunction with restrictions on domestic consumption and production'. Environmentalists have sought to use these exemptions to develop new institutions. For example, the protection of conservation-related traditional knowledge is discussed in the context of exemptions to patenting provided in Article 27(2)(b) of the Agreement on Trade-Related Aspects of Intellectual Property (TRIPs). This approach starts with the premise that the trade regime provides the framework within which to develop and articulate new principles. This approach is misguided and should be replaced by strategies that seek to develop ecological norms on their own merits and seek to create a dialogue with the trade regime.

Environmental regimes appear to be in conflict with trading rules because they often discriminate between products on the basis of environmental criteria. They impose restrictions on products, forcing their makers to include methods of production and the socio-economic context surrounding the products. International environmental laws tend to focus on the methods of production and their implications for wider environmental and socio-economic impacts—as witnessed in the case of biotechnology. These laws also tend to distinguish countries on the basis of their specific responsibilities regarding particular products. This is evident in the case of climate change and biological diversity, where the concept of differentiated responsibility has already been developed. Other principles that have been developed in the environmental field include 'prior informed consent' and the 'precautionary principle'. These measures are introduced specifically to shift institutional human behaviour towards actions that are deemed to be favourable to environmental management. But it is this biased and unjust nature that brings the two regimes into potential conflict with existing international trading rules.

The difference between the two regimes is fundamentally epistemological. Trade principles, especially those that stress product autonomy, derive their epistemological legitimacy from concepts developed in classical physics. Products are perceived as discrete entities moving unfettered in economic space. This Newtonian world-view assumes a state of equilibrium and reversibility—a reductionist perspective that does not take into account the fact that products and markets are tightly interwoven. However, attitudes are starting to change. With the rise of ecologically conscious thinking that recognizes diversity, disequilibria and irreversibility, researchers in fields such as innovation studies are increasingly using ecological principles to understand the evolution of products and markets. The challenge, now, is not how to overthrow the old principles; it is how to renew existing frameworks through a knowledge-based process that integrates institutional adjustment.

Products, processes and systems

Trade and environment regimes view the relationship between products and the wider ecological and economic environment differently. The trade regime envisages products as discrete entities that should move without discrimination through the market sphere. Indeed, one of the core principles that guide the work of the World Trade Organization is the prohibition of measures that discriminate against products on the basis of their production (except where such discrimination is allowed in accordance with GATT rules). The separation between products and processes is not a clear distinction but merely a guiding principle. There are, however, many exceptions (Howse and Regan 2000). Environmental considerations are a concern along with the impact of products and their methods of their production. This concept seeks to link the way a product is manufactured or processed to the impacts it has on the environment.

So far most of the processes and production method (PPM) approaches have been used at the national level with little impact on international trade. Interest in this subject is likely to change, however, because of the growing globalization of environmental rules. Two issues are of relevance here. Countries that adopt PPM practices that require the internalization of environmental costs may argue that their products could be rendered uncompetitive by the uneven distribution of production costs. This view may also lead to concerns about the possible use of PPMs for protectionist

purposes. Consumers, on the other hand, could apply certain values or
moral judgements and decide not to consume products whose PPMs they
deem to be harmful to the environment. Trade conflicts could also arise if
these morals or values do not enjoy universal support. It is evident from
the review of PPMs that environmental regimes could incorporate new
measures for conservation purposes into their current trading practices.
These measures, however, would need to function in a manner that does
not create trade conflicts. The effectiveness of such measures will depend
on the imposing country's market power, the level of trade dependence on
the targeted industries, and the volume and direction of trade as well as the
kinds of instruments applied.

The last two decades have illustrated the growing integration of environmental principles into the functioning of other regimes, such as trade. This
trend suggests that ecological principles have the potential to advise the
functioning of other regimes. This approach negates the need for a separate
environmental regime and lends support to the principle of integrative
responsibility. This integration is of course not limited to ecological issues.
Concerns over issues such as human rights are extending the debate from
production processes to wider socio-economic systems in which trade and
environment are only part of the equation. This development will put
greater pressure on international regimes to focus their normative work on
specific areas while participating in a wider governance network.

ENVIRONMENT, TECHNOLOGY AND PROPERTY

Environment and technological innovation

The role of technological change in international trade poses a number of
conceptual challenges. Environmentalists argue that technology is one of
the main sources of environmental damage, and activists around the world
are engaged in widescale condemnation of technological innovation. There
is no disagreement that trade, technology and environment are closely
related to each other (Johnstone 1997). What is contested, however, is how
technological change can contribute to the transition towards a sustainable
world. One view holds that slowing down technological advancement
would be beneficial for the environment. This view provides a platform for
the activities of environmental movements. An alternative view holds that
a transition towards sustainability will entail shifting towards the use of
alternative technologies that may require greater investment in technological innovation rather than less.

This debate has a wide range of implications for international trade.

First, international trade is largely dependent on continuous innovation, thus proposals that seek to slow down inventive activities are likely to be resisted. Indeed, technological innovation has been recognized as a central determinant of global competitiveness (Archibugi and Michie 1995). Secondly, the search for alternative technologies is seen as part of the logic of industrial evolution. Those who hold this view also argue that international trade, especially in new technologies, would help improve environmental management. The limits to this model are to be sought in the dynamics of technology diffusion and not in the impacts of technology on the environment.

The case of ozone layer depletion, for example, offers interesting lessons for environmental management. It was possible to ban ozone-depleting substances partly because of the promise of ozone-friendly alternative substances. This sub-regime was a direct product of public policy interventions that created incentives for developing environmentally sound products. The existence of alternative energy technologies would have a similar effect, although the climate change regime does not focus on technological substitution in the way the ozone regime does.

An innovation-based strategy for environmental management would also need to take into account the need for the wider application of new technologies (Hawken, Lovins and Lovins 1999). Ironically, a wider application is compromised by the same forces of global competitiveness that shape innovation systems in the industrialized countries. The failure to develop environmentally sound technologies is largely a consequence of resistance by vested economic interests and not an inherent attribute of technology itself. Fundamentally, this is more a result of public policy failure than it is a result of technological limitations. So far public policy in the technology-generating countries is guided by global competitiveness, which in turn defines the choice, direction and pace of technological change.

Trends in industry, however, suggest that a combination of incentives and regulations can shift technological change to meet environmental goals. Already, enterprises are responding to the growing environmental consciousness among consumers and starting to use new environmental standards. This work is promoted through the International Standards Organization (ISO) whose ISO 14000 series is being used to set voluntary environmental standards (Lally 1998).

On the whole, technological innovation is not incompatible with environmental conservation, although one can visualize a wide range of innovations that can be applied to environmental conservation. This misunderstanding drives from the widely held view that technological innovation is inherently inimical to environmental protection and the associated assumption that reductions in the pace of innovation could be beneficial to the environment. The argument defends that technological advances are inherently self-defeating because they create new and unanticipated environmental problems. Conversely, this view ignores the fact that responding to environmental challenges is a creative process that can be fostered by public policies and incentives (including intellectual property rights) that support conservation efforts. Indeed, a non-linear and systems approach would lead to new technological designs that incorporate ecological concepts such as industrial metabolism (Naray-Szabo 2000).

Property rights and environment

One of the key features of economic globalization is the extension of intellectual property rights to a wider range of product categories and the tendency to apply similar standards of protections across various categories of innovative activities—a form of normative reductionism. This process is being enforced via the implementation of the TRIPs agreement. There are two fundamental issues that arise from the globalization of intellectual property rights. The first relates to the environmental implications of this process, especially on its impacts of the conservation of biological diversity. The second issue relates to the impact of normative reductionism.

What is clear, however, is that the challenge to intellectual property rights arises from broader concerns about globalization in general. The absence of evidence linking intellectual property rights and the loss of biological diversity, for example, has not helped to reduce the concern of environmentalists because the broader considerations are still being contested. It is unlikely that research in this area will provide conclusive evidence of its impact on conservation as long as intellectual property protection is viewed as an expression of inventive activity. The issue will be settled through an examination of specific technological applications and not the existence of property rights as such.

Intellectual property regimes already provide for ways of dealing with inventions that are likely to conflict with public policies, including environmental concerns. The TRIPs agreement, for example, allows countries to bar patents for inventions that have deleterious effects on the environment. Article 27(2) of TRIPs states: 'Members may exclude from patentability inventions, the prevention within their territory of the commercial exploitation of which is necessary to protect *ordre public* or morality, including to protect human, animal or plant life or health or to avoid serious prejudice to the environment, provided that such exclusion is not made merely because the exploitation is prohibited by their law.' This provision is supported by other measures, such as the appeal to public morality as a basis for excluding inventions from patentability. The extent to which moral values are applied to patentability will vary considerably across different cultures, but there is general agreement on the core principles. Environmental criteria will increasingly become a core element in inventive activity.

Discussions on the possible impacts of intellectual property rights on environmental goals have been accompanied by debates over the scope and nature of existing intellectual property rights systems. One of the main features of globalization is the drive towards the harmonization of intellectual property rules, especially the effort to bring other protection regimes line with patent protection. The implementation of the TRIPs agreement involves this process, especially in relation to the protection of biological inventions. For the intellectual property system to work as an incentive mechanism for innovation it needs to take into account the need to promote diversity. This point is illustrated by the debate over the scope of protection conferred by geographical indications.

Geographical indications are analogous to trademarks, except that geographical indications identify territories instead of companies or brands. Article 22 of the TRIPS agreement provides protection of geographical indications that 'identify a good as originating in the territory of a Member, or a region or locality in that territory, where a given quality, reputation or other characteristic of the good is essentially attributable to its geographical origin'. The provision also prohibits the use of misleading information such as the geographical origin of a particular product.

These original TRIPS provisions set the stage for subsequent trade negotiations aimed at protecting specific geographical indications. This process has resulted in at least two issues of relevance to developing countries. The first relates to the consequences of non-compliance by developing countries whose use of geographical indications did not fall within the exceptions provided in Article 24. The second relates to the level of protection given to goods covered by the rules governing geographical indications. Currently, higher protection is reserved for wines and spirits. Developing countries have requested that the scope of protection for geographical indications be expanded to cover other goods in addition to wine and spirits. This position was first put forward by India in 1996. Developing countries, for example, have argued for the extension of higher levels of geographical indications protection to cover other products such as handicrafts and foods.

It can be argued that restricting higher protection of geographical indications to wines and spirits would not be a fair and equitable treatment of the rights and interests of WTO members. Those supporting the extension believe that this would promote the development of local products and would be consistent with the overall goals of the agreement. In the absence of such an extension, the TRIPS agreement would favour a limited number of products developed in certain regions of the world, and its role in stimulating innovation world-wide would remain open to challenge.

The extension of the geographical indications regime to other products provides a direct opportunity to integrate environmental considerations into international trade. Many of the products of the tropical world are biological in character and would receive more environmental attention if they were to occupy a prominent and recognized place in international trade. In addition to environmental goals, the regime would also contribute to the conservation of the lifestyles and cultural practices that are associated with the production of these goods. The expansion of the geographical indications regime would, in effect, contribute to the implementation of Article 8(j) on the Convention on Biological Diversity that deals with traditional knowledge. This is a significant area because of the current perception that the TRIPS agreement sits ill at ease with the goals of Article 8(j).

Future work on geographical indications will entail harmonization of practices. Some countries have specific laws on geographical indications while others rely on trademark, consumer protection, marketing and common laws, or a combination thereof. Some countries maintain formal lists while other rely on case histories. Also, some recognize place names, while others accept names that are simply associated with a place. Both practices are acceptable under the TRIPS agreement. One of the objections to extending protection to new areas is that the process would be open-ended with no limit to the kinds of products to be covered. Since the aim of international trade is to stimulate economic growth and improve human welfare, expanding the scope of coverage of geographical indications should be consistent with the overall goals of WTO. What is needed, however, is an active system for harmonizing and clarifying the technical aspects of the products.

Much of the discussion on the impact of intellectual property rights on environment assumes an absolutist view that overlooks the need to take advantage of the flexibility in the TRIPS agreement to explore areas of mutual support between the two regimes. Like in other cases, the real challenge is in the developing of national systems that seek to integrate environmental considerations into the management of private property. Many countries around the world have constitutional provisions that allow them to modify property rights to meet wider social needs, and such institutional innovations as this will in the long run help to integrate environmental considerations with inventive activities.

TOWARDS INTEGRATIVE RESPONSIBILITY

From dogma to knowledge

The debate on the environmental implications of international trade has been marked by sophisticated uses of dogma. Such uses have in some ways been inevitable given the paucity of evidence available for decision-making. Furthermore, much of the debate has been a cover for competition between nations and could be promoted as justified political actions. Where the rules of globalization provide 'winner-take-all' scenarios, dogmas become an important reference point for raising international concern or protecting one's leadership position.

The use of the precautionary principle in the global biosafety debate is an example of a concept that could serve to promote integration but has so far been advanced as a form of dogma designed to recruit support against what is seen as 'sound science'. Conversely, others have used 'sound science' to vilify advocates of the precautionary approach (a concept whose operational parameters are still being developed), yet no progress towards integration can be achieved without the use of science as a basis for risk management. Science has its limits.

The limits of science, however, demand greater investment in knowledge generation. Technological uncertainty, for example, is one of the driving forces of innovation. It can be argued that technological innovation—through product improvement and diversifications—also serves as a way to reduce technological risk, especially as capital stocks decay or the performance limits of existing systems are reached. This view would lead to the conclusion that efforts to slow down the rate of technological innovation could in itself lead to new risks. The main issue is the extent to which environmental and social goals are reflected in the design, development and diffusion of new technologies.

Ironically, it is difficult to avoid dogma because it serves important social functions. It provides a platform upon which advocates of a particular viewpoint mobilize support. But even more importantly, dogma helps to define the boundary conditions that distinguish one group of people from another; it sets the parameters for determining exclusion and social branding. Because dogma defines social boundaries, it also reduces the prospects for dialogue and design of mutually supportive regimes. Going beyond the appeal to dogma requires that genuine efforts be made to codify norms that promote integration between trade and environment.

The precautionary approach is the foundation upon which risk assessment, communication and management are done. The concept has acquired much currency in recent years because it provides a basis upon which governments can impose limits on international trade without having to provide full scientific evidence of the risks of the products in question. The precautionary approach, as outlined in Principle 15 of the Rio Declaration, states: 'In order to protect the environment, the precautionary approach shall be widely applied by States according to their capabilities. Where there are threats of serious or irreversible damage, lack of full scientific certainty shall not be used as a reason for postponing cost-effective measures to prevent environmental degradation.'

So far this approach has been used largely as a political slogan and attempts to define its policy relevance are just starting to take place. Much of its usage has been to seek a basis for challenging international trade practices that require countries to provide scientific evidence before they can prohibit the sale of a product. There are two issues that require consideration. The precautionary approach is a formal acknowledgement that scientific certainty cannot be attained and therefore decisions that require reaching these goals would postpone conservation measures indefinitely. The trade community, on the other hand, is concerned that this approach could be used as a cover for protectionism. An effective precautionary regime would need to use the best available scientific knowledge and would need to take into account public perceptions as well as the cost-effectiveness criterion spelled out in Principle 15 of the Rio Declaration. When viewed from this perspective, the precautionary approach is an umbrella concept that covers regulatory and political considerations and serves as a guiding framework. In this case, its interpretation is subject to the socio-economic context in which it is applied.

For example, countries that are faced with famine may use new technologies as part of their precautionary approach, but these same technologies may be rejected in countries where the challenges do not include increasing agricultural productivity. Scientific assessments of the nature of the problem are an essential part of the precautionary approach.

Reforming laws and institutions

Global issues are largely a result of national experiences, which are articulated at the international level through sovereign activism. This activism is either based on proven practices at home or is an effort to share the risks of experimentation. Indeed, there are many of forms of activism where the risks of experimentation are transferred entirely to other countries, but what is relevant for purposes of this discussion is an indication of the extent to which environmental principles are integrated into national practices. The existence of such practices makes it possible to reach international consensus.

One of the key features of the current global governance system is bureaucratic inflation: too many organizations, conventions, processes and conferences chasing too few good ideas. Much of the international diplomatic circuit is devoted to ensuring that there is consistency in the way these ideas are expressed and implemented. Those who work to promote consistency also help to transfer the idea from one regime to another. This inflation is reflected in the extensive overlap between the activities of various international organizations and is assisted by the sovereign nature of these institutions. The search for commonalities in environment and trade faces these same challenges because of the potential overlap between the two regimes.

International institutions play an important role as a mechanism for global learning by sharing experiences. It is through such global learning and experience-sharing that effective codification can be done. This view has implications for international legal instruments that are anticipatory in nature. These instruments, however, can only provide the framework within which experiments can be carried out but cannot be expected to show concrete results except in very specific areas. Indeed, treaty bodies are guidance instruments and the best indicator of their effectiveness is the extent to which they have influenced behaviour in the performance of other institutions, especially at the national level.

Much of the debate on trade and environment has been about the choice of regime. Environmentalists have argued, and with justification, that they cannot trust the trade regime to effectively address their concerns. This concern is borne out by the fact that various bodies set up under the GATT in the early 1970s to address environmental issues remained dormant. That these organs did not function may be because trade regimes define environment as an externality (Arrow *et al.* 1995). The early 1970s was a period when the GATT was engaged in a series of negotiations aimed at addressing issues, such as tariff barriers, which were central to its functioning and therefore paid little attention to environmental and other issues. In addition, there was no other regime that was strong enough to force the GATT to take environmental issues seriously. Today there is a wider choice of regimes, and recent debates on biosafety and toxic chemicals show that environmentalists would prefer to address the impact of trade on environment in regimes where they have greater political control.

The issue that arises from this observation is: should non-trade international agreements address trade issues? Environmental conventions will address trade-related activities if these activities undermine environmental goals. But the way these conventions address trade issues will be determined by wider considerations in international law. What is emerging, however, as illustrated by the biosafety discussions, is a clear difference between institutional authority (for example, having a dispute settlement mechanisms) and public opinion (as expressed by consumer and environmental organizations). This makes the issue of choice of regime a political one.

An alternative to this scenario is to move towards mutual recognition of the principles developed in other regimes and the creation of mechanisms for regime harmonization. There are various options open to the international community in dealing with this. The first is to establish forums that bring different regimes together. Such forums have already been created to deal with issues such as labour and forest management. The value of such forums is limited to the exchange of information and the identification of areas of common interest or concern, but they cannot serve as a substitute for the internal functions of specific regimes. Their role, however, will increase as global governance becomes more complex.

One of the key issues in the codification and harmonization of environmental criteria and indicators is to determine how to define the scope of various international regimes. Underlying this dilemma are conceptual differences that reflect political objectives and aspirations. Since the release of *Our Common Future* the international community promoted the principle of integrative responsibility and sought to embody environmental considerations into development objectives. This concept guided the negotiations that resulted in the adoption of Agenda 21, the work programme of UNCED.

Integrative responsibility has, over the years, gained in currency and now represents one of the most successful reform efforts in the United Nations system. Nearly every international organization has sought to link environment to its development activities. Similarly, many government ministries at the national level have mirrored this development. However, this development has been seen as a threat to the nascent efforts of environmental agencies and institutions which have in turn sought to establish a separate regime purporting to offer specialized guidance on environmental conservation.

Advocates of a new global environment organization allege that global efforts to protect the environment are stalled in part because of 'weak institutional structure'. They speculate on the significance of institutional problems and provide no evidence to support the view that environmental conservation will be improved through the creation of a new United Nations agency. A viable proposal for a new agency requires a clear and compelling organizing principle, credible design concept and realistic implementation plan. They offer none of these; instead, they rely largely on arguments based on administrative efficiency.

First, such advocates attribute lagging global environmental efforts to the fact that environmental tasks are fragmented and performed by too many uncoordinated agencies and treaties. Second, they bemoan the lack of enforcement mechanisms in most existing treaties. Third, they say the agency would help transfer environmental technologies and finances to developing nations. And finally, they appeal to the need for a body that would serve as a counterweight to the WTO. None of the reasons has a sound basis.

It is true that transboundary environmental problems—all of which have national sources—require concerted international action. This is already being done through a number of international treaties and organizations. A new agency will not replace existing efforts but will add another layer of bureaucracy to an already complex network of treaties and organizations with no global constitutional structure for effective coordination. Each of these treaties and organizations is sovereign and derives its authority from its governing body and responds to its internal political demands. The example of biological diversity shows that the creation of an umbrella treaty only provokes dormant institutions into action and increases the transaction costs of global governance.

Here are a few examples: acting on global warming requires national action to meet commitments under the Kyoto Protocol under the United Nations Framework Convention on Climate Change—a new agency will add little to this process; setting standards on marine pollution should build on the work of the International Maritime Organization; promoting guidelines for ecosystem management should support the work already initiated under Convention on Biological Diversity; work on environmental impact assessment in institutions such as the World Bank should be given greater legislative authority. There are numerous other efforts that need to be supported and strengthened, not denigrated and undermined by political activists.

The assertion that consolidating existing international organizations and secretariats of conventions will result in a stronger and more effective agency is based on a misunderstanding of how international institutions function. Secretariats of conventions and international bodies receive their instructions from their governing bodies. Administrative efficiency should not be confused with programmatic coherence. Secretariats of conventions cannot be combined without the approval of their respective governing bodies. Advocates of the new agency have not indicated how they plan to deal peacefully with the divergent governing bodies. Attempts to control the message of the different conventions can only undermine their effectiveness.

The perceived competition for finances is in part a result of the failure by many governments to pay their dues, which is often prompted by concerns

over bureaucratic inflation. There is no evidence that the situation will
be different under a new organization, and, furthermore, many of the
agencies dealing with environmental issues focus on distinct but complementary functions that should not be collapsed under one behemoth. This
simple fact is lost to those who look at institutions as if they were func-
tionally similar. The differences may appear trivial but their operational
implications may be profound.

For example, some of the convention secretariats have operational functions while others are limited to supporting the operations of the conferences of the parties and their subsidiary organs. Combining normative and
operational functions will quickly result in a dysfunctional body, as illustrated by the organizational difficulties experienced by international
organizations created through the combination of pre-existing bodies and
committees. An example of this is the United Nations Educational,
Scientific and Cultural Organization (UNESCO).

Agencies such as the International Civil Aviation Organization (ICAO)
owe much of their organizational effectiveness to functional clarity. It is
clear that ICAO is a standards-setting organization; it is not clear what the
functional focus of UNESCO is. It is clear that the WTO is a rules-based
organization; but such functional clarity cannot be attributed to the
United Nations Environment Programme (UNEP). Functional clarity
cannot be achieved merely by reducing the number of activities that an
organization is engaged in; indeed, many of these activities are self-similar
or do not vary with change in scale or size. Functional clarification is essentially a result of rigorous consensus-building around specific scientific or
technical questions.

Environmental problems are diverse in character and require specialized
institutional responses. Where coordination is needed, governments can
do that without creating a new bureaucracy. There is, however, an urgent
need to share experiences and lessons, codify principles, promote guidelines and set new standards. But this is just what global treaties on climate
change, biological diversity, endangered species and control of desert
growth were created to do. Many of them are already doing this without
the perils of centralization.

It is true that most environmental agreements lack effective enforcement
mechanisms. One of the reasons is that governments cannot agree on how
they should work. Drawing on their experiences with the World Bank and
the International Monetary Fund, many developing countries are concerned that a new environmental agency would only become another
source of conditions and sanctions. What is needed is greater support for
research, training, education and public awareness in developing countries
in keeping with the Earth Summit commitments.

More has to be done at the national level. If governments promote greater compliance with domestic environmental laws, they will find it easier to direct it towards international cooperation. What is perceived as deficient global environmental regulations is really an indication of poor domestic housekeeping.

They should ratify and implement the agreements they have negotiated and should promote the integration of environmental concerns into other agencies. Where there is a genuine gap in the regime, they should seek to reach agreement through existing bodies and where there is none they should create one. Yet they should resist the tendency to create new agencies simply because existing ones are not working effectively. The case for a new agency should be made through an open and democratic process involving all governments, relevant international institutions and civil society organizations.

Most developing nations cannot meet their obligations under various environmental treaties. They say this is partly because the richer nations have not honoured their commitments to assist them with technology and finances. There is no guarantee that the new agency will perform better in this regard.

In addition, developing nations have consistently argued that environmental conservation should be promoted as part of their overall economic goals, as agreed by UNCED. Creating a new agency focusing on environment over development, as is proposed, would amount to reneging on this historic agreement and will antagonize developing countries. Alternatively, the new agency will be forced to include development considerations and will simply duplicate existing agreements on sustainable development.

The claim that a new agency would serve as a counterweight to the WTO is equally flawed. The WTO undoubtedly needs to take environmental issues seriously, but this would be more effectively done by integrating environment into trade activities and not simply by creating a new agency. Deciding on how to deal with the workload in the WTO is a matter that is internal to the organization and cannot be solved through a separate regime.

To justify the claim to a separate regime, a number of concepts have been developed which include 'deference'. This idea seeks to clarify the roles of the WTO and MEAs. On the surface, the concept of 'deference' appears to provide a legitimate basis for reducing possible conflict between WTO and MEAs, but on close examination, the concept appears to be an attempt to request the WTO to cede part of its jurisdiction to the environmental regime with little indication that this would result in a reduction in the presumed conflicts. Even more importantly, this process would undermine the integrative responsibility of WTO towards environmental goals, which are clearly reflected in its mandate. Deference would in practice mean that WTO would leave global environmental decision-making to MEAs despite the fact that MEAs would still continue to use—and legitimately so—trade-related instruments to meet their objectives. Because of the difficulties and uncertainties associated with the interactions between environment and trade, such a move could lead to a new class of conflicts related with determination of competence and jurisdiction. The success of such an approach presupposes perfect knowledge on the boundary conditions between trade and environment, a matter that is evidently a logical impossibility.

Another approach based on integrative responsibility would seek to promote greater recognition of environmental consideration in trade decisions through the establishment of appropriate standards, criteria and indicators. This requires a stronger and more active Committee on Trade and Environment in the WTO. So far governments have not given the requisite attention to the CTE and as a result its role is not taken seriously. It can be argued, however, that the performance of the CTE is a reflection of the overall performance of the environmental regime. A greater focus on normative development in other environmental bodies would help strengthen the CTE by proposing new standards that could be integrated into the trade regime.

The existence of credible forums would also help to increase the sensitivity of trade regimes to environmental concerns through institutional learning. Indeed, the WTO incorporates a wide range of normative standards that were developed in other regimes and organizations and were consolidated through a process of global learning, but the environmental regime would continue to use trade-related measures to address environmental goals. What is critical is the level of interaction and coordination between the two regimes. It is important to stress that such interactions and coordination should start at the national level with efforts to incorporate environmental considerations into economic activities in general and trade in particular.

It can be argued that such an approach would result in overlaps between the two regimes. Overlaps are not necessarily a negative development; indeed, a certain measure of jurisdictional redundancy is essential in ensuring that environmental goals are pursed through a variety of ways. It is critical to ensure that the measures are complementary and not contradictory. This will be achieved through continuous dialogue and experimentation in the two regimes, not by simply drawing arbitrary boundaries between trade and environment.

Furthermore, the differences between the approaches taken in the two regimes will be determined largely by their normative approaches, which are unlikely to be similar. So far, the trade regimes are clearly rules-based while the environmental regimes are still experimenting with a variety of normative standards, none of which has emerged as a core guiding framework with the functional expression of the concept of non-discrimination in the trade regime. The absence of a dominant guiding framework should not be seen as a weakness of the regime but a feature of the complexity of environmental governance as well as the nascence of the regime itself. Norms emerge through long periods of experimentation. They give form to institutions, not the reverse. This is partly why the desire for a world environment organization is frustrated by the lack of a common vision on feasibility.

CONCLUSION

Environmentalism is driven by a sense of urgency that is not quenched by calls for time and adjustment, while international trade is driven by age-old dynamics and patterns that do not change overnight. Between these two contrasting approaches lie some fundamental rigidities about industrial structures and attitudes. Perceptions tend to change faster than societies are able to modify social behaviour, a process that is usually inter-generational. Industrial structures, which define the character of produc-tion, are usually slow to alter and tend to settle into certain reproducible patterns and trajectories. Punctuation from these trajectories takes a com-bination of changes in public opinion and consumer taste (which environ-mental movements can influence) and technological transition (which the private sector is better suited to effect). Maybe integrating trade and envir-onment will need to start with new alliances between environmental movements and entrepreneurs who recognize the importance of intercon-nections in nature and economy.

At the moment, what is lacking is the requisite intellectual and political leadership needed to guide the dialogue. But for such leadership to emerge the international community will need to recognize the importance of integrative responsibility and set up institutions that mirror the way the real world works. It will take visionaries to focus global attention on gen-erating the knowledge needed to guide new forms of global governance that integrate trade and environment. But as the world waits, it is import-ant that ongoing experiments in environmental governance, especially at national and regional levels, be given the political space to mature (Clark 2000). Therein lie the seeds for more robust and integrative governance systems.

REFERENCES

Adams, J. (1997). 'Globalisation, trade, and environment', *Globalization and Environment*. Paris: OECD.

Archibugi, D. and J. Michie (1995). 'The globalisation of technology: a new taxonomy', *Cambridge Journal of Economics*, 19: 121–40.

Arrow, K., B. Bohlin, R. Costanza, P. Dasgupta, C. Folke, C. S. Holling, B. O. Jansson, S. Levin, K. G. Maler, C. Perrings and D. Pimentel (1995). 'Economic growth, carrying capacity, and the environment', *Science*, 18: 520–1.

Bhagwati, J. and T. N. Srinivasan (1997). 'Trade and the environment: does environmental diversity detract from the case for free trade?', in J. Bhagwati and R. Hudec (eds.), *Fair Trade and Harmonization: Prerequisites for Free Trade?* Vol. 1: *Economic Analysis.* Cambridge, MA: MIT Press.

Clark, W. (2000). 'Environmental globalization', in J. Nye, and J. Donahue (eds.), *Governance in a Globalizing World*. Washington, DC: Brookings Institution Press, 86–108.

Cole, M. A., A. J. Rayner and J. M. Bates (1998). 'Trade liberalization and the environment: the case of the Uruguay round', *World Economy*, 21(3): 337–47.

Ekins, P. (1997). 'The Kuznets Curve for the environment and economic growth: examining the evidence', *Environment and Planning*, 29: 805–30.

Eskeland, G. and A. Harrison (1997). 'Moving to greener pasture? Multinationals and the pollution-haven hypothesis'. Policy Research Working Paper No. 1744, Washington, DC: World Bank.

Esty, D. (1994). *Greening the GATT: Trade, Environment, and the Future*. Washington, DC: Institute for International Economics.

GATT (1971). 'Industrial pollution control and international trade'. July. Geneva: GATT.

Grossman, G. M. and A. Krueger (1995). 'Economic growth and the environment', *Quarterly Journal of Economics*, 110(2): 353–77.

Hawken, P., A. Lovins and L. H. Lovins (1999). *Natural Capitalism*. London: Earthscan.

Howse, R. and D. Regan (2000). 'The product/process distinction—an illusory basis for disciplining "unilateralism" in trade policy', *European Journal of International Law*, 11(2): 249–89.

Johnstone, N. (1997). 'Globalization, technology, and environment', *Globalization and Environment*. Paris: OECD.

Lally, A. P. (1998). 'ISO 14000 and environmental cost accounting: the gateway to the global market', *Law and Policy in International Business*, 29(4): 501–38.

Naray-Szabo, G. (2000). 'The role of technology in sustainable consumption', in B. Heap and J. Kent (eds.), *Towards Sustainable Consumption: A European Perspective*. London: The Royal Society, 67–73.

Nordstrom, H. and S. Vaughan (1999). *Trade and Environment*. Geneva: World Trade Organization.

Odman, A. N. (2000). 'Using TRIPS to make the innovation process work', *Journal of World Intellectual Property*, 3(3): 343–73.

OECD (1997). *Globalization and Environment*, OECD Proceedings. Paris: OECD.

Repetto, R. (1993). *Trade and Environment Policies: Achieving Complementarities and Avoiding Conflicts*. Washington, DC: World Resources Institute.

Sampson, G. P. and W. B. Chambers (2000). *Trade, Environment and the Millennium*. Washington, DC: Brookings Institution Press.

Taylor, A. and C. Thomas (eds.) (1999). *Global Trade and Global Social Issues*. New York: Routledge.

Tussie, D. (ed.) (1999). *The Environment and International Trade Negotiations: Developing Country Stakes* (International Political Economy series). New York: St. Martin's Press.

World Commission on Environment and Development (1987). *Our Common Future*. Oxford: Oxford University Press.

Xing, Y. and C. Kolstad (1998). 'Do lax environmental regulations attract foreign investment?' Mimeograph, Santa Barbara: University of California.

3

Social Movements as Problematic Agents of Global Environmental Change

Steven Yearley

BY the end of the old millennium, social movement organizations (SMOs) had become the most popularly acclaimed and, in many respects, trusted agencies advocating global environmental change. They had won widespread public admiration because of their daring and heroic undertakings, because of the verve and symbolic acuity of their actions and because they seemed to be in the vanguard of environmental change. Of course, commentators noted that governments and inter-governmental agencies might have more power to set and influence environmental standards, that companies might be making the greatest impacts on the environment, that it was often scientists who identified possible environmental problems which were 'off the radar' of environmental groups, and that the daily consumer choices of the industrialized world's massed citizens and commuters might outweigh their efforts. All the same, social movements represented the quintessential environmental actor. In cultural terms, environmental organizations stood for the environment in a way which the Environment Minister, the collected scientists of the Intergovernmental Panel on Climate Change or Shell simply could not. Moreover, those movement organizations which focused on issue of *global* environmental change seemed particularly successful; in the late 1980s through to the early 1990s—around the time of the Earth Summit—they were rewarded with disproportionately rapid growth and cultural cachet (see McCormick 1991: 152–5 who cites Friends of the Earth, Greenpeace and the World Wide Fund for Nature (WWF) in this regard). And their market prominence within the NGO sector has largely continued.

At the same time, social movements commanded the attention of social scientists and commentators. For one thing, social movements and the associated movement organizations appeared to confound expectations.

Far from politics as usual, social movements indicated how successfully and how enduringly people could be organized—or organize themselves —around non-conventional political objectives. Standard economic and political theories did not anticipate that people 'ought' to mobilize so successfully around a diffuse political objective such as global environmental improvement. In the UK, where movement organizations succeeded even more thoroughly than elsewhere, several groups had memberships in the hundreds of thousands, with the largest easily exceeding memberships of political parties and coming well within an order of magnitude of the total membership of the Union movement.

Secondly, social movements appeared effortlessly and beguilingly innovative: they pioneered new forms of campaigning designed to maximize publicity. Greenpeace have perhaps become the masters of this practice, generating widely circulated images of high-seas heroics. In the case of the Brent Spar protests in 1995 (aimed at preventing the ocean disposal of an oil-storage platform called the 'Brent Spar'), so successful were they in their command over the production of news images that the television industry was led to reflect on its information serfdom; virtually all the video coverage of the ageing oil installation was supplied by Greenpeace itself. Comparable creativity was shown by roads-protesters in the mid-1990s who developed techniques for delaying highway construction first by occupying the trees which were to be felled, then by tunnelling under the path of construction equipment. Tree camps powerfully symbolized the solidarity between protesters and the aspects of the natural world they were trying to protect, but the tunnels represented a special daring since it was the very fragility of structures which ensured that constructors (probably) would not dare drive construction equipment over the occupants. Jasper has recently written of the *Art of Moral Protest* (1997) and it is this kind of phenomenon whose artfulness he salutes. In recent years, other environmental activists have shown similar creativity, whether reclaiming the streets by holding fairs on motorways or cycling in concert to disrupt the flow of motorized traffic.

Finally, social movements appeared effective; many campaigns with which they were associated (even if they did not inaugurate them) were successful, including limitations on whaling, reductions in acid emissions from factories, vehicles and power stations and limitations on sea-dumping. Yet, despite the growing social scientific and journalistic interest in social movements, it is extraordinarily difficult to make an audit of movements' activities. For one thing, movements have long-term impacts which are necessarily hard to measure. Environmentalist campaigns are typically just one element in a wide range of factors affecting decision-making. In discussions with environmental campaigners in the UK, I have heard them characterize the running down of civil nuclear power as a successful campaigning 'outcome', but policy shifts were also in part ascribable to the examination of costs prompted by the privatization of the bulk of the UK electricity-supply industry and to the disastrous handling of the Chernobyl reactor accident. Furthermore, social movements and movement organizations have every reason to exaggerate their achievements while their opponents are correspondingly inclined to play such accomplishments down. Finally, part of movements' success has resulted in movement organizations winning access to formal advisory structures and to intergovernmental panels, so that the very definitions of official action and movement influence blur.

If an assessment of their impact remains elusive, so too does an agreed analysis of their status. For some commentators, social movements are principally the result of the work of moral entrepreneurs. Skilfully deploying the resources of publicity generation and fund-raising, issue entrepreneurs attract supporters, possibly ones whose socio-economic position makes them responsive to so-called progressive issues (a position persuasively sketched by Berger 1986). On this view, supporters are lured to the issues rather than discovering them for themselves. On a more Hegelian view, popular for nearly three decades in Continental Europe, only some issues have the historical potential to engender movement activity. These are ones which identify a 'true' collective interest. In some sense, these movements are expected to follow the idealized pattern of the labour movement's development, systematically pursuing the group's collective interests and identifying a common enemy. In this spirit, Giddens has suggested that true social movements can be expected to coalesce around what he terms the 'institutional dimensions of modernity', including capitalist accumulation and the industrial transformation of nature (1990: 158–63). Similarly, in a recent review (1999), della Porta and Diani have insisted that social movements should not be reduced to the activities of the movement organizations. It is appropriate to speak of movements only when there is a broad background level of support, not when activity is limited to organizations alone. There is thus a continuing tension in analysts' minds about the relative importance of SMOs and the movements they represent.

Hence my objective in this chapter is not to carry out an audit, but instead to draw attention to a series of themes which impact on the ability of movements and movement organizations to operate as agents of *global* environmental change in the new millennium. I will classify this analysis around four themes: expertise and authority, solutions orientation, global representativeness, and imagining futures.

EXPERTISE AND AUTHORITY

Though it is in many ways obvious, the dependence of the environmental movement for its credibility and authority on scientific and technological expertise is often stressed insufficiently. The principal claims of other social movements are typically on fairness or rights. Women's movement activists could see no reasons why women should earn less for the same work than did men; they didn't understand why women should be expected to handle the bulk of childcare when men were also parents. Of course, occasional science-like claims about natural differences between women and men sometimes entered into the debate; certain kinds of discrimination might be underlain by biological differences. But these were seldom thought to be enough to justify the *status quo*, and were indeed arguments of last resort. Similarly the legal obstacles to gay couples adopting children have been contested on rights grounds. The scientific fact of men's (current?) inability to carry children was not allowed to be a consideration since adoption was available for women in heterosexual partnerships who, for biological reasons, were also unable to bear children. Equally, the LBG (lesbian, bisexual and gay) movement's unease about claims for the genetic basis of gayness—whatever these claims' scientific merits—is indicative of the subordinate status of scientific arguments to the gay rights case. By contrast, environmental claims are typically about matters of supposed fact. The climate is, or is not, becoming warmer. Hormone-mimicking pollutants do or do not threaten to cause hormonal changes in wildlife and humans. Sea-floor dumping of oil installations risks contamination of the benthic environment or not. Sowing genetically modified crops will or will not lead to genetic contamination.

On the face of it, movement leaders and campaigning organizations with a popular mandate face specific kinds of difficulty in mobilizing scientific and technical arguments. In particular, it is hard to combine responsiveness to one's supporters' views with a commitment to identifying what is technically correct. It may just be that what one's supporters think is environmentally important is not scientifically urgent (or vice versa). Initially, that is around one hundred years ago, nature conservation groups were unaffected by this dilemma because they were societies of and for natural scientific observation. In groups such as the Royal Society for Nature Conservation (now called the Wildlife Trusts), the technically trained effectively set the conservation agenda. But with the rise of broad-based environmentalism in the 1970s this difficulty became manifest. Loosely expressed, supporters were inclined to adopt a broadly environmental world-view, worrying about the release of pollutants and the diminution of resources. But to achieve advances in pollution abatement and related legislation, to win court cases about planning consents, or to enter into negotiations with regulators, more precise calibrations of environmental harm had to be demonstrated. Campaigners came to be at least as sensitive to the information demands of their opponents as to the views of their supporters. Worse still, the need for increasingly technical cadres in these organizations threatened to recreate Michel's iron law of oligarchy at a technical level; the professionalized scientific staffs of the SMOs became distant from the supporters on whose funding and occasional participation they depended (see Yearley 1993).

Central though science was to continuing campaign success, it was moreover apparent to movement activists that demands for scientific proof were often used by official agencies to thwart the advancement of environmental reforms. Official agreement to act as soon as the evidence was incontrovertible all too often amounted to a commitment to equivocate for an indefinite period. Movement actors found that scientific reasoning was both necessary and yet ideologically suspect. Part of the answer to this difficulty was enthusiastic support for the precautionary principle, since this provided good grounds for opposing nearly all forms of novel pollution until evidence of lack of harm could be provided. But, of course, precautionarity is a rather imprecise criterion. As many natural scientists never tire of observing, it is impossible on approximately Popperian grounds to *prove* a lack of harm; it must always be possible that some hitherto-unconsidered mechanism could render a technology or technique harmful. Put more realistically, it is clear that the precautionary principle demands skilled interpretation on every occasion of use; otherwise, novel wind turbines, solar collectors and other environmentally benign technologies would not get over the hurdle of precautionarity.

These difficulties are severe enough when one is dealing with the role of science in the national context of an industrialized country. However, the problem that social movements have experienced in generalizing from these organizational foundations is that global science is conspicuously harder. For one thing, there are serious pragmatic barriers to taking part in global science. The resources needed to participate in global climate change analysis, for example, are very great and, as Boehmer-Christiansen has pointed out in a number of papers, have effectively been concentrated under the auspices and guidance of the World Meteorological Office (WMO) (see 1994*a*; 1994*b*; 1996). The WMO's World Climate Research Programme sets the limits to recognized contributors to knowledge. Though not so obviously 'big science', even international biodiversity has steep entry barriers. To make compelling proposals about where to concentrate spending on biodiversity conservation one needs standardized surveys and inventories; these are costly, estimated last decade to cost over

$200 million (Yearley 1996: 137). Secondly, it is hard to agree levels of pre-cautionarity world-wide. Different cultures and varying levels of socio-economic development mean that precautionary risks will be evaluated differently in different contexts. Social movement activists cannot expect the precautionary principle to draw a line in the sand for them since the principle necessarily admits of so many interpretations.

The practical impediments to social movement participation in advanced global environmental science are clearly severe. But there is a complementary problem related to the perceived failings of top-down expertise. Major environmental policy problems, notably difficulties about how to handle the threat of BSE and of how to regulate genetically modified crops, have lately made it clear to policy-makers and the public alike that technical expertise alone is insufficient to control urgent prob-lems in a credible manner. Expert bodies often appeared to be unjustifiably sanguine about the scale of environmental problems. And, as a result, public confidence in the reassurances of government-appointed experts declined. If expertise is seen as suspect, policy-makers cannot assume the public will support measures just because they are pronounced to be in line with the best expert opinion. In response to this credibility problem, com-mentators increasingly argue that there is a role for public participation in the certification and quality control of expert knowledge (see Yearley 2000). Typically, the claim is not that citizens should have a voice simply because of their democratic entitlements, but because they bring expertise which is either distinct from or more inclined to integration that that of discipline-based experts. Indeed, people's everyday or working experience may qualify them to be a certain kind of expert alongside technical special-ists. For example, slaughterhouse workers may know more about the practicalities of stripping potentially infected meat out of carcasses than officially appointed experts on spongiform encephalopathy. The prag-matic argument is also offered that technical recommendations which have been subject to some form of participatory public consultation are more likely to win public support.

Environmental NGOs have shown themselves to be supportive of such initiatives when they happen to favour the campaign trend of the organ-izations themselves. But they are none the less keen to retain a sense of their own authoritative expertise. Of course, NGOs have acquired considerable credibility 'capital' since they have a record of erring on the side of caution and public health, but they have shown little enthusiasm for exploring new models of expertise. Indeed, the newest manifestations of ecological social movements have tended, to a large degree, to bypass expertise. Roads pro-testers' tactics work precisely by changing the situation rather than win-ning arguments about it. The instrumental aim, insofar as there is one (and

I don't say this in a snide manner), is to increase the cost of road construction to the point where it is unattractive, rather than to show that environmental valuations have been too low or that the supposed benefits of the new road will be undermined by excessive traffic growth.

Though their claims to expertise have been publicly bolstered by their record of partisanship in favour of the public interest, environmental SMOs have not to date been good at establishing novel forms of credibility-building. At the same time, the demands of truly global expertise make it hard for movement organizations to boast of conventional expertise in international policy-relevant science. Their principal successes have been in publicizing international scientific knowledge and, as with CITES (the Convention on International Trade in Endangered Species of Wild Flora and Fauna, dating from 1973, where WWF has played a large role), assisting in tracking implementation. The strategy of winning recognition as expert bodies in a national context, which many large environmental groups have cultivated, is not necessarily well adapted to authoritative global campaigning.

SOLUTIONS ORIENTATION

The difficulties experienced in relation to expertise are compounded in an ambivalence exhibited by environmental SMOs in relation to adopting—to use the (ugly) term of art—a solutions orientation. The early 1990s appeared to offer a key turning-point in the development of environmental social movements (see Rose and Melchett, this volume). Endorsed by the Earth Summit in Rio in 1992 (see Strong, this volume), the concept of sustainable development seemed set to transform the business of activism around environmental issues; the role of SMOs seemed set to switch from that of outsiders offering a critique of advanced-industrial society to insiders performing a central role as part of the officially sanctioned solution. Environmentalists could come in from the cold because all development now had to be sustainable; this meant that everyone—governments, industry, international bodies and SMOs—should be pulling together for the same objectives. In principle at least, environmentalists were indispensable to plans for a sustainable society and were to be offered a key role in the reform and re-development of society's core socio-economic activities.

At the same time it appeared that environmental problems, even the most intractable ones, could be tackled. The hole in the ozone layer had been acknowledged and was now likely to heal itself in the coming decades. Institutional arrangements for recycling and waste reduction advanced beyond previous expectations. Advocates of ecological modernization argued that firms could benefit economically from cutting emissions and waste. The nuclear industry was in retreat and the scope for renewable energy looked attractively large. It began to seem that environmental management was all about balancing trade-offs and the language of environmental economics became the dominant mode for describing such trade-offs with optimum rationality (even among many NGOs).

In this context, climate change occupied a key role. Clearly the problem was vast, uncertain and complex. Huge vested interests stood in the way of arriving at solutions before excessive and perhaps irremediable warming took place. But there was still a cautious optimism that a solution could be found. The Intergovernmental Panel on Climate Change (IPCC) was established to provide an international forum for establishing reasonably certified scientific claims about the scale and nature of the problem, and negotiations began about how the burden of coping with the issue could be shared in a practicable but also reasonably equitable way. While it would be wrong to say that environmentalists and policy analysts were comprehensively optimistic, their pessimism was at least bounded.

Some unease disturbed this rough consensus: roads protesters argued that governments were not treating environmental protection anything like seriously enough within transport planning. Indeed, many believed that sustainable road-building was oxymoronic. But even these arguments could still be handled within the dominant discourse of sustainable development. The problem was that governments were failing to implement their in-principle commitment to sustainable development in the case of road transport; they simply needed to be embarrassed back into line.

By the end of the millennium, however, this temporary alignment of forces in the UK around the concept of sustainable development had been ruptured; environmental campaigning had returned to its oppositional status and Lord Melchett of Greenpeace was (however briefly) imprisoned. Genetically modified (GM) foods were the occasion for this change. The environmentalists' 'victory' over GM, though still not secure, was outstanding. Though the leading NGOs had been preparing their case against GM technology for nearly a decade, the policy success came very quickly. Corporations, most notably Monsanto, which looked so secure and powerful, were speedily brought low. Many US farmers switched out of the technology for fear of losing European export markets; pension funds and other institutional investors moved out of GM stock, drastically reducing the companies' value; and supermarkets in the UK and France in practice became the regulators of GM purity in their respective countries.

But this stunning reverse has to be seen in the light of the fact that this was a familiar form of campaigning. Interview and case-study analysis conducted in the early 1990s indicated ambivalence about sustainable development among environmental organizations (from Friends of the Earth and the Green Alliance to the CPRE, the Council for the Protection of Rural England) from the start. Some respondents worried that official agencies and companies would subvert it, others that, strictly interpreted, sustainable development set minimum standards of survivability only. But there was a more fundamental unease about whether it was possible to move from an oppositional stance to a position of being partners in finding solutions. In part, misgivings on this score were driven by suspicion of former opponents; concessions had only been won through hard opposition before and there was no evidence that the commercial pressures which favoured short-termism would be any different now. Such worries were compounded because SMOs' strategy in the past had precisely been not to 'own' the problems. The nuclear industry, for example, has always been keen to present the amassed nuclear waste as a 'national' disposal problem. Repeated attempts were made to involve environmental organizations in devising solutions to this problem. The same held true for other kinds of hazardous waste where disposal firms routinely ran up against locally based opposition, typically driven by NIMBY (not-in-my-backyard) considerations. But social movement organizations were reluctant to become embroiled in such ventures. Their attitude was that the waste was in no sense their responsibility. It was the company or the industry which had produced it and there was no reason why the voluntary body had any obligation to help the company out of its fix. In the terms of the old joke about travel directions, the NGOs affirmed simply that they wouldn't have started from there.

It is telling also to note that probably the other single largest environmental issue of the 1990s, at least in the European context—mad cow disease (BSE)—witnessed little participation by NGOs. The media were more important than NGOs in bringing this to the public's attention. The political action by other EU member states and by the Commission itself were the factors which highlighted the extent of the problem and the severity of the social impacts. And it was the supermarkets and other food retailers which played the role of working out credible social techniques for holding or rebuilding public confidence. Of course, NGOs used the problem as an occasion for promoting ideas about the change to organics or the need for de-intensification. They stressed lessons about the need to separate industry interests from the regulatory authority. But, given the role which the BSE case is thought to have had in alerting European consumers to the potential harms of 'mad maize' (and other 'mad' GM crops as they have been styled in France), the lack of social movement involvement in working out practicable solutions is striking.

Given these two grounds for reluctance—an unwillingness to 'own' the problem and uncertainty about whether the polluting leopards have changed their spots—social movement ambivalence about offering solutions to global environmental problems is understandably limited. Of course, there are solutions of a sort aplenty in simply no longer doing so many of the bad things. At the launch of the UK government's policy document on sustainable development in the mid-1990s, the memorable response of Friends of the Earth was to call for less worry about what sustainable development was and more emphasis on ceasing things known to be unsustainable.

An acute and instructive form of this difficulty in an international context arises in relation to another disputed matter, population. For many in the North, particularly those in right-leaning administrations, growing population levels (especially in the South) are self-evidently an environmental problem. Development campaigners from the South dispute this notion; they argue that the North's excessive consumption is far more damaging to the planet than the South's admittedly numerous but very low-consuming citizens. In the present context, it is the near-silence maintained by the North's leading green NGOs which is particularly noticeable. Green Parties which are obliged to have policies across the board have at least been forced to confront the question of what their ideal population level for, say, Germany or the UK would be; they have also had to set out their attitudes to immigration into Western Europe and so on. But the North's environmental NGOs have very largely avoided campaigning on this issue even though it surfaces in all major international confrontations between policy-makers of North and South—as, for example, at the Earth Summit in 1992. This brought about the ironic situation in which, at the time of the UN population summit in Cairo in 1994, Jonathon Porritt (former director of Friends of the Earth in London and a major influence on the British Green Party for many years) could write a newspaper article calling on UK environmental NGOs to be less timid about the population issue (Porritt 1994). To coincide with the Cairo conference, he called on them to approach the then minister for Overseas Development (Baroness Chalker, a Conservative), a woman who—he suggested—was open to arguments about the need to work through the empowerment of women in the Third World. He felt NGOs should be more strident in calling for internationally agreed policies to cut the global rate of population growth. In this case too, therefore, SMOs were reluctant to offer public pronouncements about solutions. The NGOs' relative silence is explained, I suggest, by two factors. First, Northern NGOs' existing technical expertise has, to date, not been concentrated in this area since it has not been an issue for campaigning within the North. Thus inertia inclines them to silence on an issue of great practical importance. Silence motivated by humility is compounded by a recognition that the subject is highly contentious and that, whatever view one takes, one is likely to antagonize as many people as one attracts. Pragmatic judgements favour silence too (Yearley 1996, 205–11).

For wholly understandable reasons, environmental NGOs have been at best ambivalent about becoming involved in helping established authorities resolve society's environmental problems. SMOs have not necessarily trusted their new, would-be 'partners'; nor have they wanted to become associated with environmental problems which they did not cause. Such ambivalence can be expected to be no less in the case of global environmental issues.

GLOBAL REPRESENTATIVENESS

In addition to difficulties with summoning global expertise and in pioneering solutions to global problems, environmental social movements experience difficulties in claiming international representativeness. Within their own territories, social movement organizations may have an approximately democratic or mandate-based legitimation. Sometimes NGOs invoke the sheer numbers of members as surrogates for the popular legitimation of their action. On other occasions they may call on opinion polls to show that the majority of the population endorse, say, their worries about climate change. Or, as when Greenpeace activists de-contaminated fields of GM crops in summer 1999, they turn to broader democratic notions of the public interest. But at a world-wide level this is much harder. The wealthy and internationally powerful environmental SMOs are clearly from the North. The need to retain a Northern membership base sometimes skews their interests in favour of the characteristic concerns of their supporters but, even when it does not, their view of the environment may not be shared in the South. They cannot as readily claim a popular mandate in Southern countries.

One practical way of speaking for everyone is to try to identify universal standards. Such standards are clearly attractive to movement organizations; differential safety standards have legitimated dumping and the export of wastes in the past. But the appeal of universalism may have hidden limitations. In a paper with Kevin Stairs (a lawyer employed by Greenpeace), the consultant Peter Taylor discusses the example of possible unintended consequences of Greenpeace's commitment to end ocean dumping of sewage. He suggests that a position worked out in relation to the North Sea and other industrialized seas is not necessarily appropriate in the case of

South-East Asia, where there is little industrial contamination of sewage: 'sea dumping could be [environmentally] justified if the costs of land treatment were unrealistic' (1992: 133). On this view, sea dumping may be the less bad option in certain contexts; there is no guarantee that a universal rule will be appropriate the world over.

Official international agencies have sought to use the discourse of science to speak directly and unequivocally to global environmental problems. Science offers a language of universality. One molecule of carbon dioxide is comparable to any other; once conversion factors are applied, all ozone-depleting molecules can be rendered comparable. Some commentators from the international relations literature have interpreted this move as an essentially progressive one, arguing that epistemic communities fostered around scientific expertises allow technical groups in different countries to forge alliances. This route has commonly been regarded with some unease by NGOs since they are aware that these equivalences may be contestable or even prejudicial to Southern interests. The case of the costings of lives in the South, associated with option appraisal for greenhouse gas abatement measures, was perhaps the most celebrated instance of this. In an attempt to work out for the IPCC how much should 'rationally' be spent on abating climate change and how much it made sense to merely adapt to climatic alterations, a figure was needed for the loss of well-being attributable to the possible human casualties of climate-induced environmental changes. In turn, this required an economic value being attached to the loss of income from lives lost and so on. According to the techniques used, a life in Bangladesh came out to be 'worth' just a few per cent of the value of a US or European life. This 'technical' conclusion was met with indignation, particularly from Southern NGOs. However, once social movement groups deny themselves this technical route to universality, SMOs face difficulties in finding a sufficiently robust alternative legitimation for world-wide policy prescriptions. They find themselves in a precarious position where they have neither a democratically mandated nor a technically secured purchase on the 'correct' global policy stance.

IMAGINING FUTURES

My final observation is that social movement organizations have not to date been successful in elaborating an agreed sense of what an attractive global future might be. The flawed and openly technocratic ideal of sustainable development was minted directly out of policy-makers' discourses. It drew an artful compromise between some nations' demand for development and others' insistence on environmental protection. As noted above, environmental SMOs have had misgivings about that image from the start. But movement organizations have neither agreed nor clarified their alternative.

Given movement actors' concern with combating damaging practices, some commentators have seen ecological modernization as the route implicitly followed by leading environmental SMOs (for example, Sonnenfeld 1999). Ecological modernization assumes that there can be a progressive rationalization of environmental policy. As Mol helpfully expresses this idea: 'Ecological modernization indicates the possibility of overcoming the environmental crisis while making use of the institutions of modernity and without leaving the path of modernization. The project aims at "modernizing modernity" by repairing a structural design fault of modernity: the institutionalized destruction of nature' (1995: 37). While NGOs have not, typically, embraced this perspective in an explicit way, Sonnenfeld sees their pressure on industry and government as tantamount to implicitly pursuing an objective of ecological modernization. Reforms and legislative changes are demanded which will improve environmental policy performance and ensure that the worst pollutants and the most damaging practices are phased out.

Though a modernization perspective can be adopted as an interpretation of how environmental policy should be, for authors such as Mol it stands as an account of how social practices in fact are (see Mol 1997: 140). The assertion of such authors is that, in specific ways, commercial development and rising environmental standards can go hand-in-hand. Cases such as those of low-odour (or otherwise less dependent on organic solvents) paints, or less and less environmentally damaging pesticides become paradigmatic for this analysis. There is, so to speak, a ratchet effect which drives environmental reform in a single direction and makes it cumulative. Moreover, once one country establishes demonstrable environmental improvements through the pursuit of a policy, there is enormous pressure on others to follow. If limitations on acid emissions result in improved air quality or if one country reduces demands on landfill by obligatory recycling measures, others will (in some strong sense) have to follow. The policy's 'betterness' is indubitable (see Weale 1992).

In many respects this is a comfortable ideology to which to subscribe. It tolerates a good deal of variation in terms of detailed policy prescriptions and offers the prospect of environmental advances within the framework of existing social institutions. But, ecological modernization cannot guarantee that enough reform can be achieved to avert major ecological problems. The claim is a weaker one than that, amounting to the idea that technological development, industrial policy and environmental

improvement can pull in the same direction. In this regard, the environmental movement resembles the feminist movement: it has no agreed
conception of what would amount to a sufficient transcendence of the
status quo. But, unlike the feminist movement, it considers that the present
situation is continually worsening. The prospects for devising an agreed
global image of the desired future are correspondingly meagre and the
movement risks accommodating to unproved gradualism.

It is precisely in this context that links between environmental campaigners and anti-capitalist/anti-globalization protesters make most sense.
The informally organized but commonly well-attended protests against
the workings of the World Bank, International Monetary Fund and World
Trade Organization which developed in the late 1990s and which shad-
owed high-profile meetings of these various bodies can be read as an
expression of the conviction that business as usual for capitalism can only
lead to greater exploitation and environmental despoliation. Many environmentalists and environmental groups have drawn succour from these
protests, sensing that there is a global outrage at the harms which universal
capitalism may cause. But these protests share with modern global environmentalism the problem of knowing (or even conceptualizing) what
alternative they favour. Without a clear alternative, the protesters risk
being 'bought off' with the few concessions they may win or risk falling
out among themselves about their longer-term objectives. In this sense, the
anti-capitalist protests seem to mirror closely the predicament of global
environmental campaigners.

CONCLUDING DISCUSSION

In this chapter I have tried to do something for which social science is
perhaps ill equipped. I have sought to take the evidence of trends in the
behaviour and stance of environmental SMOs and, from these, to project
possible future orientations of these organizations. Overall, my argument
has been that, though at the turn of the twentieth century environmental
NGOs are indeed the quintessential environmental actor, the strengths
and strategies that have served them well to date will not necessarily equip
them for a leading role in global environmental campaigning in future
years. At the global level they face problems of representativeness; they
operate with a notion of expertise which is nearly as rigid as that of official
'authorities' and they face organizational problems in moving towards a
future- and solutions-oriented position. Of course, this is not a 'scientific'
prediction. Social movements have constantly surprised commentators by
their inventiveness and self-transformational abilities. But, despite the

clear successes of the environmental movement in the last forty years, we cannot be sanguine about SMOs' future credentials; they remain problematic as agents of global environmental change.

REFERENCES

Berger, Peter L. (1986). *The Capitalist Revolution: Fifty Propositions about Prosperity, Equality, and Liberty*. New York: Basic Books.

Boehmer-Christiansen, Sonja A. (1994*a*). 'Global climate protection policy: the limits of scientific advice—Part I', *Global Environmental Change*, 4 (2): 140–59.

Boehmer-Christiansen, Sonja A. (1994*b*). 'Global climate protection policy: the limits of scientific advice—Part II', *Global Environmental Change*, 4 (3): 185–200.

Boehmer-Christiansen, Sonja A. (1996). 'Political pressures in the formation of scientific consensus', *Energy & Environment*, 7 (4): 365–75.

della Porta, Donatella and Diani, Mario (1999). *Social Movements: An Introduction*. Oxford: Blackwell.

Giddens, Anthony (1990). *The Consequences of Modernity*. Cambridge: Polity.

Jasper, James M. (1997). *The Art of Moral Protest: Culture, Biography and Creativity in Social Movements*, Chicago: Chicago University Press.

McCormick, John (1991). *British Politics and the Environment*, London: Earthscan.

Mol, Arthur (1995). *The Refinement of Production: Ecological Modernization Theory and the Chemical Industry*. Utrecht: International Books.

Mol, Arthur (1997). 'Ecological modernization: industrial transformations and environmental reform', in Michael Redclift and Graham Woodgate (eds.) *The International Handbook of Environmental Sociology*. Cheltenham: Edward Elgar, 138–49.

Porritt, Jonathon (1994). 'Birth of a new world order', *The Guardian*, 2 September: 8–9.

Sonnenfeld, David A (1999). 'Social movements and ecological modernization: the transformation of pulp and paper manufacturing', paper presented to the International Studies in Planning Seminar, Cornell University, 7 May.

Stairs, Kevin and Peter Taylor (1992). 'Non-governmental organizations and the legal protection of the oceans, a case study', in Andrew Hurrell and Benedict Kingsbury (eds.) *The International Politics of the*

Environment: Actors, Interests, and Institutions. Oxford: Oxford University Press, 110–41.

Weale, Albert (1992). *The New Politics of Pollution.* Manchester: Manchester University Press.

Yearley, Steven (1993). 'Standing in for nature: the practicalities of environmental organizations' use of science', in Kay Milton (ed.), *Environmentalism: the View from Anthropology.* London: Routledge, 59–72.

Yearley, Steven (1996). *Sociology, Environmentalism, Globalization.* London: Sage.

Yearley, Steven (2000). 'Participation and the public's discontents with expert knowledge: a review and case study', *Public Understanding of Science,* 9: 105–22.

4

Global Citizens: Campaigning for Environmental Solutions

Chris Rose and Peter Melchett

THIS chapter deals with three linked issues. First, the nature of modern campaigning, with particular reference to the work of Greenpeace and the solutions they offer. Second, the role of Greenpeace and other non-governmental organizations from the not-for-profit sector. Third, the challenge and opportunities created by 'globalization' and what this means for global governance from an environmental point of view.

CAMPAIGNING AND SOLUTIONS

For some years Greenpeace has argued that 'solutions' have moved to centre stage in the work of pressure groups, as they used to be known. The formative role of environmental campaigning organizations was to draw attention to problems, but by the 1990s, finding and demonstrating solutions, and getting them applied, became much more important (see Yearley, this volume).

This has proved a long and hard road. Indeed, the gap between what can be done and what is being done has, if anything, widened. This is mainly because the technical potential has improved while, in Britain at least, implementation has moved much more slowly. It was once famously said of an incompetent British government that this is an island built on coal and surrounded by fish, but still it manages to run out of both. Similar things could be said today. The government has patently failed to protect fish stocks but that can be conveniently blamed on the EU Common Fisheries Policy. But no such excuse will wash on energy. Britain's wave energy resource is more than 70 times the UK electricity demand. Britain's wind resource is also vast. Offshore wind could meet Britain's entire electricity demand three times over. Against this, the government's unattained

target of 10 per cent for renewable electricity is simply pathetic. Contrast
Britain with Denmark, which is phasing out fossil fuel use in electricity
generation and is on course for generating 50 per cent of its electricity from
wind alone by 2030. Little wonder Denmark is reaping the benefits in
terms of engineering jobs in wind turbines, an industry in which it is world
leader. The story in Germany and the Netherlands is similar: yet Britain is
far, far windier.

The reason for this seems to lie overwhelmingly in the personal beliefs of
so many of Britain's political, industrial and indeed chattering classes. The
conservatism, for which this country is infamous, coupled with attitudes
ranging from distrust to active dislike of anything to do with the environment, strangles most far-sighted environmental initiatives at birth. For
example, it is conventional wisdom in UK government circles that solar
photovoltaics will remain simply too expensive to form a major part of a
move away from fossil fuels. Quite apart from other considerations, this
ignores the very rapid pace of cost reduction. The cost of solar panels has
dropped a hundredfold in the last two decades. Why is this relevant to the
government? Because the government needs to give a lead. To facilitate, to
encourage, to regulate.

The suburbs are the most ignored, and frequently vilified, areas of our
country—lost between our love of the countryside and concern about
inner cities. The suburbs could become the largest power station in Britain.
Fitting passive solar, solar thermal or solar photovoltaic energy systems
could convert the suburbs from a huge energy consumer into Britain's
largest power station—but a dispersed one which would also be a buffer
against energy costs and fuel poverty for the old and poor, and against failures of the grid system. Consumers with pv or combined heat and power
plants can earn money in times of surplus, by exporting electricity to the
grid, as indeed our office in London does.

Obviously this could also make a very significant contribution towards
reducing use of fossil fuels and meeting the stricter reduction targets that
will inevitably follow the current Kyoto and domestic UK government
target. The government's own sustainable development indicators paper
(Anon 1999) selects CO_2 emissions as a key indicator and then notes that
the CO_2 target is expected to be broken as emissions rise beyond 2010.

Britain has no significant government-funded or organized solar housing programme of the sort under way in continental countries at the same
latitude. The Netherlands has a programme to put solar pv on 100,000
homes by 2010, and Germany has a similar programme for 100,000 solar
roofs. The European Commission called for solar to be installed on half a
million roofs by 2010 which it is estimated will lead to a market worth
some 10 billion dollars, creating 100,000 new jobs. Britain still lags behind,

despite studies for the Department of Trade and Industry that suggest solar pv alone could provide between two-thirds to all the electricity used in the UK. In addition, a report for Greenpeace UK by Cambridge Econometrics and Forum for the Future has found that a publicly funded investment programme in renewable energy (scenarios whereby renewables account for 10 per cent and 15 per cent of electricity generation by 2010) would secure considerable environmental benefits, essentially at no cost to the economy.

Turning to another equally practical subject—the use and pollution of water—there is again an abundance of technical solutions that are simply not being used. Here it is very clear that it is the institutional conservatism of the water industry, coupled with the timidity of Whitehall, that is to blame. At the start of the twenty-first century, Britain is still building longer sea outfalls to convey human excrement into the seas around our shores, often with very minimal treatment. This policy directly flows, if that's the right word, from the invention of the flush water closet, which created the first large-scale freshwater pollution disasters in London in the nineteenth century, and then closed Parliament with the smell. London's great sewers were built, and the resulting outfall created a pollution disaster down the Thames. Sludge treatment followed and killed off inshore fisheries. So then the authorities started dumping by boat, taking the sludge out into the North Sea. Scientists grew increasingly concerned about the long-term build up of pollutants and the spread of viral and bacterial disease among fish and other life. The public were more and more alarmed about the implications for human health. Greenpeace campaigned against it, and secured a ban on sea dumping in the 1980s. For the most part, the final result of this and the associated attempts to implement the EU Bathing Water and other European directives was longer and longer outfalls, taking the pollution away from beaches and deeper into the sea.

These are false solutions. They will inevitably lead to more long-term problems. The interaction of science, the politics of risk and technology serves to perpetuate a problem rather than deliver a solution. Sewage contains persistent organic pollutants (known as POPs), such as phthalates, alkyl phenols and dioxins. These are not usually recorded in water quality assessments and mostly remain unaffected by sewage treatment systems. Along with heavy metals, these chemicals are implicated in birth defects, behavioural impairment, cancers and interference with the immune system in marine mammals and human beings. Britain is signatory to the Washington Convention which sets out to deal with the problem of POPs—so far with little result. Pumping sewage out to sea or down rivers, after first mixing in industrial and domestic waste, is no way to deal with this problem. The resulting ecological interactions of these inputs are so vastly complex that they almost defy scientific investigation. In the 1980s Greenpeace overturned conventional wisdom about substance-by-substance pollution controls on liquid wastes by demonstrating with gas chromatography that many entirely new pollutants were being formed as discharges that made their way in to the sea, quite outside the scope of the models on which the licences were based.

In these circumstances politicians will always be able to say that there is no conclusive (simple, one-dimensional) evidence that links particular chemicals to particular problems. This is an illustration of what the German sociologist Ulrich Beck has called 'organized irresponsibility'. In this instance, science cannot do the job for you. Instead you need intellectual tools like the precautionary principle, to enable you to deal with uncertainty. An excellent study of the different dimensions of pre-caution is contained in a study for the EC Forward Studies Unit by Andy Stirling of the Science and Policy Research Unit at Sussex University (Stirling 1999). Stirling recognizes that policy-making means confronting 'incertitude'—which is composed of risk, uncertainty, ambiguity and ignorance. These are very different factors and cannot be swept away under one carpet labelled 'science' or 'risk assessment'. Stirling goes on to point out that broad appraisal of new technologies, and the dimensions of the issue brought out by pressure groups actually means *better* science than the narrow 'sound science' approach of most governmental and corporate assessments.

It is perhaps the hubris of the educational systems of industrial society that leads us to imagine we are capable of effectively analysing and 'dealing with' such interlinked scientific, technical and political problems. It is time to recognize, instead, that many of these issues are simply too difficult to be resolved within the sorts of time-scales generated by commercial and public projects designed to meet human needs. The probability that we will get it right is very low indeed. The probability that we will create long-term problems that can only be detected a long way down the line, is rather high.

The only practical alternative is to use our more holistic knowledge of the functioning of ecosystems to design-out such problems in the first place (cf. Odum, this volume). Working with the design, or grain, of nature rather than against it is the best bet in seeking industrial systems that do not cause long-term, widespread ecological problems. We are, after all, dealing with natural functioning systems which have been refined through mil-lions of years of evolution—a design subsidy that we cannot compete with. To achieve better living we need to get away from fixing the symptoms to fixing the causes, using more intelligent 'clean production' and closed-loop systems that do not give rise to waste in the first place.

Both the case of energy and the case of water pollution demonstrate how the pursuit of 'solutions' cannot be separated from policy and analysis of 'problems'. Even the most comprehensive packaging and bundling exercises by industry have yet to supply for sale a sustainable lifestyle package along with its own atmosphere, hydrological cycle, 3-D living space and key life nutrients such as nitrogen. So we are here dealing with the politics of public goods, and government is essential in delivering such solutions.

As well as working to reform a political understanding of science, Greenpeace works with technologists and businesses to develop and realize technological innovations. Our thinking has been that because of the power ceded to corporations by governments (for good or for bad), because of the enormous impact that a particular choice of technologies can have on the environment, and because of the powerlessness that consumers feel when acting individually, our particular role can be to take individual technologies and harness public engagement to help force or cajole companies into making them a reality. Where the private sector goes, the public sector is then often more willing to follow.

Our experience with technological solutions projects goes back to the 1980s. It started really with the Montreal Protocol and the development of what is now known as 'greenfreeze' refrigeration technology in 1992. CFCs were being phased out, but the speed of the phase out was largely determined by what the chemical industry said was feasible. The political authorities running the Montreal Protocol and the governments of countries party to the Protocol simply accepted the word of industrial giants such as Dupont and ICI when they said that the only technical alternatives to CFCs were the 'softer' but still ozone-destroying HCFCs, and HFCs which did not destroy ozone but were extremely potent greenhouse gases. The most important uses of these gases were in refrigeration and chilling. The refrigeration equipment manufacturers were not very interested as the gases are only a tiny part of the cost of a product such as a fridge. Moreover their engineers had trained and grown up using halocarbon type gases and knew very little about alternatives.

In the spring of 1992 Greenpeace brought together scientists who had extensively researched the use of propane and butane as refrigerants, with an East German company DKK Scharfenstein. The company had been producing refrigerators for fifty years and was the leading household appliance manufacturer in the former East Germany. After reunification, however, it faced severe economic problems and was due to be closed down. The meeting between the scientists and DKK Scharfenstein resulted in the birth of greenfreeze technology for domestic refrigeration. Greenfreeze refrigerators use hydrocarbons for both the blowing of the insulation foam and the refrigerant, and they are entirely free of ozone-destroying and global-warming chemicals. Greenpeace successfully campaigned to gather tens of thousands of pre-orders for the yet-to-be-produced new refrigerator from environmentally conscious consumers in Germany. This overwhelming support from the public secured the capital investment needed for the new greenfreeze product, and at the same time, salvaged the company and saved the jobs of its workers.

The major household appliance manufacturers, who had already invested in HFC-134a refrigeration technology as the substitute for CFCs, at first claimed that the greenfreeze concept would not work. However, upon realizing that the first completely CFC-, HCFC- and HFC-free refrigerator was about to come on the market, and recognizing the market appeal of a truly environmentally friendly refrigerator, the four biggest producers—Bosch, Siemens, Liebherr and Miele—gave up their resistance to the hydrocarbon technology, and introduced their own line of greenfreeze models in the spring of 1993. The greenfreeze technology spread rapidly. Hundreds of models of greenfreeze refrigerators are now on sale in Germany, Austria, Denmark, France, Italy, Netherlands, Switzerland, and Britain (including the Iceland 'Kyoto' range, which makes the explicit link to climate change). All of the major European companies are marketing greenfreeze-technology-based refrigerators, which has become the European standard. Production began in China in 1996.

Greenfreeze is technically superior in performance to HFCs (cheaper, more energy efficient and easier to use) but still faces strenuous lobbying by HFC manufacturers such as ICI. Even the UK government relies for policy formulation on advice from companies such as March Consulting, although March has worked for the European Fluorocarbon Committee, a chemical industry lobby group for HFCs! March often stresses the benefits of HFCs and the problems associated with alternatives, such as hydrocarbons and ammonia. Even so, greenfreeze is gradually making more ground in Britain, and there is progress in Argentina, India, Indonesia and Cuba. In Japan the market leader, Panasonic, has a greenfreeze prototype. But in the USA HFCs remain dominant.

The pace of and limits to market change demonstrate that government regulatory action is still required. Recently the Danish government announced measures to eliminate HFCs by 2006. Britain's Minister of the Environment, Michael Meacher, stated at a meeting with Greenpeace recently: 'We don't want to give the point of view that HFCs are there for a long time. The policy of the UK government is that we want to phase out HFCs as quickly as we can.' If commitment is given then this can be done, for instance 100 per cent of German industry has converted to hydrocarbon technology, and in China over 50 per cent of production is now greenfreeze, and in total there are over 40 million greenfreeze units in the world today. Without this campaign, far larger amounts of CFCs and certainly HCFCs and HFCs would have been used, and released in to the atmosphere. Greenpeace undoubtedly succeeded in changing the trajectory of the industry, but there is still some way to go.

Another case tells a similar story. The manufacture of paper using chlorine bleaches creates a very wide range of pollutants, including large numbers of dioxins. In the early 1990s the Greenpeace toxics campaign set out to prove that pulp and paper manufacture was possible without any chlorine at all. After our argument was rebuffed, Greenpeace resorted to securing a supply of non-chlorine bleached paper. In fact it was the first time that such pulp had been sourced and that the technical difficulties had been overcome in order to produce commercial quantities of paper from it. Greenpeace went on to produce a publication with the paper, only it was not a Greenpeace publication but a facsimile of *Der Spiegel*, Germany's most prestigious political commentary. When confronted with the evidence of *Das Plagiat* which had also been mailed to their own subscriber list, coupled with the gift of several large rolls of chlorine-free paper, the publishers gave in and converted to non-chlorine-bleached paper.

The campaign against chlorine bleaching has succeeded in converting much of the industry to ECF paper—which is 'elemental chlorine-free' and significantly reduces the total load of pollutants. Fewer users, however, have opted for totally chlorine-free or TCF paper. Like greenfreeze and HFCs, this example emphasizes that while commercial and market mechanisms may create rapid and innovative change where industrial–political regulations were deadlocked, they are relatively unreliable at delivering a complete solution. For that, government regulation is still required.

In the UK we have campaigned to persuade users of PVC, another chlorine compound with significant toxic by-products in manufacture, use and disposal, to adopt alternatives. We have secured the backing of major companies like Lego, Mattel and Nike, and succeeded in 'persuading' a reluctant government to accept an alternative to PVC for the roof of the Millennium Dome. The substitute—teflon—converted it from a two-year structure to a 25-year structure: one of its few selling points it seems! It is noteworthy that it was Greenpeace and not the UK government who put in the time and effort to locate the alternative. It is far from being a perfect material, as Teflon also creates pollution, and in fact better substitutes have since become available, partly as a result of that campaign.

Another innovation introduced as a result of a Greenpeace campaign is the development of a PVC-free credit card. Until this card was developed in cooperation with the Co-op Bank, all credit cards contained PVC.

Typically, such innovations involve developing new applications for existing technologies. The popular media image of a scientist leading technological change by making an astonishing discovery is rarely true. The reality is that there is huge gap of implementation: vested interests, a lack of leadership or finance, and professional and institutional conservatism are all holding back environmental solutions.

Perhaps the most obvious examples are from the renewable energy and car sector. We have already mentioned solar, wind and wave energy. Greenpeace has been extremely active in promoting the adoption of renewable energies for the last decade. We have taken UK minister Michael Meacher to see offshore wind farming in Denmark. We are working with the local community in Islay to install wave power. We installed solar pv on the UK Department of the Environment (as it then was) and on the roof of the house of the Australian prime minister. We solarized a school in Crete and a batch of homes in Silvertown, East London. We toured Britain to explain the technology, using purpose-built solar façades that can run washing machines and do other 'hard work'. The Greenpeace Environmental Trust has also for some years funded innovative solar photovoltaic work at Imperial College in London.

But none of this will succeed simply by advocacy. Solutions are not implemented mainly because there is vested interest in maintaining the problem. There is no clearer example than fossil fuels. The oil companies have the know-how and the finance to convert the world's energy systems to renewables tomorrow. BP was a stakeholder in one well-known study which shows that if solar photovoltaic production was scaled up to a 500 megawatt plant (for a fraction of BP's annual investment in oil exploration), it would be cost-effective against fossil-fuelled electricity today. The reality is that BP's business, and their share price, is based more on new exploration and continued growth in use of oil, and that is why they press ahead with pumping more from existing fields like the North Sea, and opening up entirely new 'provinces' like the Atlantic Frontier. So long as they can do this, and continue pumping volume, they will not change to renewable energy companies, nor will they develop the technologies beyond the present token level, nor will they cease lobbying for business as usual.

This is why we continue to oppose companies such as BP on the North Slope in Alaska, where it aims to open up the Northstar development, and on the Atlantic Frontier where they and others would like to see the oceans around St Kilda and Rockall opened up as a massive new oil field. Greenpeace campaigning has resulted in a legal victories that have slowed and may yet stop development in both of these arenas, and we have succeeded in splitting the oil industry, with BP and Shell for example, leaving the Global Climate Coalition (the GCC). The GCC is a mainly US lobby group that worked to prevent governments agreeing a climate convention at Kyoto, and now works to prevent action to reduce climate change. More recently Ford has also left the Global Climate Coalition, and it is heartening that major manufacturers such as Ford are developing fuel cell engines. It is disheartening that many of them seem to plan to use fossil fuels as their source of hydrogen when renewables could do the job!

There is so much that can be done with existing technologies, but there is a danger that a lack of government direction will simply allow existing polluting systems to coexist alongside new, cleaner ones. Without any new technology, fuel consumption of cars in mass production today could be at least halved. Greenpeace clearly demonstrated as much in the early 1990s, with our conversion of a small Renault standard production model car to a SmILE—standing for Small, Intelligent, Light and Efficient—that used half the fuel of the original model.

THE ROLE OF GREENPEACE IN CIVIL SOCIETY

After the 1999 Seattle WTO (World Trade Organization) meeting, the *Economist* magazine railed against what it called 'uncivil society', by which it meant the protestors. It might better be said that it was the WTO which needed civilizing. The protestors were not the cause of the problem. It is unfortunately typical of the treatment of these issues in the news media that it is easier to report the street clashes than it is to report what is going on inside and behind the scenes. As Michael Meacher, the British Minister for the Environment, remarked, 'What we hadn't reckoned with was the Seattle Police Department, who single-handedly managed to turn a peaceful protest into a riot.' He compared the officers involved in the 'over-zealous police security operation' to 'Star Wars-style storm-troopers'. It is the way the WTO has been conceived, set up and run which is the long-term problem. The WTO exemplifies the worst excesses of global, but effectively unaccountable, institutions which have no connection with any human value except the making and celebration of money. As such it throws a harsh light on the issue of how society operates, what NGOs are for and what NGOs actually do.

By 'NGO' we are talking about environmental and other social NGOs, not industry or business groups which may be non-governmental but are essentially private, or representatives of private interests. In contrast, NGOs from the not-for-profit or voluntary sector are, by and large, vehicles that represent the public interest. Most literally they are vehicles to represent interests of the public that are not represented in the fabric and

institutions of civil society. In some cases they are as such transitional—
and may disappear or be eclipsed as government institutions, the educational system, or maybe the private sector take on their role, or as formal
political parties incorporate their ideas or functions. In other cases, they
may co-exist. In any event it is not so much their history or future but what
NGOs do now, that we want to focus on.

At the most basic level, environmental NGOs exist because there is a
social deficit in society. Greenpeace operates as an inspiration, as an active
conscience that goads and encourages industrial society to put right at least
some of its dysfunctional relationship with nature. It operates in that mar-
gin between what society knows it ought to do, and what it actually does.
That is, essentially, where its legitimacy comes from. Therefore, it is not
representative legitimacy, it is moral legitimacy. This moral legitimacy,
and the strict moral boundaries within which we operate, form the platform for Greenpeace's distinctive direct actions. Most of the daily activities of industrial society—how we work, travel, enjoy ourselves, what goes
on while we sleep, what our pensions and wages earn as they rest in the
bank—all cause environmental damage rather than repair, cause loss rather
than gain in the ecological accounts. Most of what most companies do, is
an environmental negative. Most government activity and the function of
most government departments, are environmental negatives. It is the
mission of groups like Greenpeace to try to redress the balance, and to
inspire society to do likewise on a bigger scale. Greenpeace, as one film
maker said, is a little light in the darkness.

The NGOs that make up the environment movement are winning most
of the arguments but as yet their ability to win the war—to determine real
outcomes—is still extremely weak and patchy. The environment is still
being rapidly and widely degraded. Despite significant progress—including change in the thinking of many business leaders—the odds are still
heavily stacked against us. It is said for example that for every NGO
lobbyist in Brussels, the EU capital, there are at least 100 business lobby-
ists. In trying to help make up for the failure of government, politics and
business, NGOs take on many roles. They sometimes educate, they sometimes advocate, and they often provide agency for individuals. As we have
already said in discussing examples of Greenpeace's work, they research,
break new ground in politics and science, and develop solutions that commerce does not. NGOs often become shadow government functionaries.
Many international treaties and conventions would simply collapse or
achieve nothing without the active intervention of NGOs. NGOs frequently act as intermediaries and diplomats where governments will not,
and in ways that business simply does not know how to. NGOs are not
perfect instruments free from interests, but compared with private busi-

ness they are. Because they do not have the profit motive, NGOs can be trusted in the social sphere in a way similar to government when it is functioning well. Business cannot be. Most of all, however, NGOs exist to change society in a particular way. They have a social purpose, and in the last decades of the twentieth century, the environment movement has been the clearest example of that.

Of course redressing the balance on such a grand scale involves unsettling a few interests. Hence the periodic cries to investigate the accountability and legitimacy of NGOs. These cries invariably emanate not from the 'normal public' but from one or more of three sources. First, from multinationals or other business interests, and particularly those who have been subject to campaigns or scrutiny. Second, from politicians in government who have been inconvenienced by NGO campaigns. Third, from commentators in the media who take on the mantle of champion for one of the other two groups. It all misses the point. NGOs are there because the systems of government and the mechanisms of civil society are still failing to halt environmental destruction. The question is not whether NGOs are somehow accountable or representative of society as a whole—of course they are not and, if they were, they might simply replicate the failure to deliver results! The real question is why the machinery of government, the process of politics and the activities of commerce continue to destroy environmental quality when their leaders ostensibly espouse its protection. NGOs arise from two essential democratic freedoms: the freedom to assemble or of association, and freedom of speech. They are, to a large extent, a symptom of a functioning civil society, and its ability to heal and improve itself. This brings us to the third element: the challenge and opportunities created by 'globalization' and what this means for global governance from an environmental point of view.

GLOBALIZATION AND GOVERNANCE FOR THE GLOBAL ENVIRONMENT

The conventional, or perhaps one should say the clichéd, point of view is that globalization threatens the environment and those who would protect it. A political apocalypse is in progress, in which sinister legal machinations will be used to cleanse societies of regulations and practices that protect the environment. The WTO is frequently held up as physical evidence of this phenomenon. In the other corner are those who believe that globalization and freer trade is going to bring untold economic benefits, that the market is capable of delivering everything worth having and that there is too much government, and that anything which might stand in the way of free trade reaching in its purest form into every nook and cranny of life, must be swept aside.

Most politicians who advocate the second view are to be found in Washington DC, and it is one dimension of the unfortunate divide that has opened up between the political cultures of Europe and the United States. Few European or Japanese politicians would advocate untrammelled operation of the free market, but there are many politicians and quite a few business people in the United States who seem to believe that globalization is the process by which the world is adopting a US-style capitalist economy. There are quite a few others elsewhere who fear that this is exactly what is occurring! The truth is more complex. For one thing there is a lot of confusion between globalization and the spread, or not, of particular economic models and of free markets in particular.

There is no doubt whatever that the spread of technologies is global. While this may bring threats, on balance it is probably good for the environment, in so far as there are technical solutions to industrial problems. Clearly, for example, it is better for the environment if you walk to work rather than using a car. But if you do use a car, one that runs on hydrogen generated by solar power is going to be far preferable to one that runs on petrol. The spread of the Internet and other forms of new media are, so far, a liberating and broadly democratic influence. The effective dissemination of information about environmental problems and solutions has to be a good thing. We should also remember that long before globalization appeared to be an economic phenomenon, it was an ecological reality. The spread of heavy metals, organochlorine chemicals, the build up of greenhouse gases and the hemispherical reach of acid rain, have gone on for most of the last 100 years.

Although the protests at Seattle got the headlines, the underlying failure was nothing to do with the protestors. There was a genuine deadlock between nation-states over what to do about the terms of trade. A part of that involved the environment and the other unresolved issues about people's rights to curtail trade and economic activities so that they maintain the quality of life and the environment (cf. Juma, this volume). The UK government and others may or may not be insincere when they advocate an ethical or environmental reform of the WTO but they are certainly bowing to the *realpolitik*, that the voters don't want free trade as much as they want a good quality of life.

The fact that the United States and Monsanto tried to impose GM foods on Europe and failed is a sign that new forms of politics are at work, and that globalization will not necessarily mean a licence to every technology and practice no matter what the consequences. Of course NGOs played a key role in that rejection. First when Monsanto tried to force GM upon the

European consumer, second when the US government took up its case at the G8 and the WTO. The geopolitics are fascinating: the United States economy is sufficiently big and self-contained to resist doing what the rest of the world wants it to do. But it is not economically big enough to make the rest of the world fall into line with what it wants. Hence the cognitive dissonance that often seems to fall upon the more insular of Washington politicians. However, geopolitics are only half the story. A new form of politics is in operation, one that does not always involve politicians from the 'political classes' or those who are politicians in the formal political process. This is 'new politics', as commentators such as Andrew Marr have termed it (Marr 1995).

In the aftermath of the WTO it is easy to forget what happened earlier to the proposed Multilateral Agreement on Investment. That, it is generally acknowledged, was killed off by 'new politics' and the opposition of NGOs using the Internet to organize. Greenpeace has been involved in many such cases although few of them receive a lot of media coverage, mainly because the press (particularly in the UK), is myopically besotted with the village news of the old political system—the adjoining parishes of Whitehall and Westminster. One very clear, and well publicized example was the campaign to prevent the sinking of the Brent Spar, the redundant oil installation run by Shell. It was not government policy or political debate which altered Shell's plans (which had themselves been approved by the UK government with no opposition from other governments around the North Sea). Instead it was resolved by a company choosing to listen to its customers rather than to a government. Greenpeace of course played a strategic and catalytic function but, without the public revolt against Shell, there is no doubt that the Brent Spar would have been sunk.

The Brent Spar also illustrated some other notable aspects of the 'new politics'.

- It concerned risk and the politics of risk (concerning the distribution and creation of risk)—despite the fact that this was largely denied by the conventional political system.
- Government policy was changed in line with the public feeling afterwards. Both nationally and internationally as Britain, along with twelve other governments in the region, signed an international treaty banning further dumping.
- It involved the use of images with iconic significance rather than ideological argument. One observer wrote afterwards that it was: 'A handful of chaps on a lilo taking on the entire Western economy—and with it the biggest piece of litter in the world . . . an incident crammed with dramatic polarities and symbolism of the most unsubtle kind.'

- Rather than voting with a ballot box it involved voting with consumer choice. Free market theorists ought to have loved it for the 'frictionless' ease with which consumers could make their displeasure felt by switching to another brand of petrol at no cost to themselves.
- It involved the use of the Internet to inform. During the Spar campaign Greenpeace's website carried sometimes minute-to-minute developments well ahead of the conventional news media, and visitor numbers were among the highest anywhere on the web at that time.

Both the Brent Spar and the struggles with Monsanto had all the attributes of a 'citizens arrest' through new politics. However, neither is any form of governance. Of course there is no global governance as such. There are those who wield enormous power, such as Rupert Murdoch, OPEC, the US Congress and the companies gathered at the World Economic Forum in Davos. But they are usually unable to use it to dictate events beyond a relatively narrow sphere around their own operations. Then there are the governments—organizing themselves through the EU or the UN or the Bretton Woods Institutions and their descendants. But none of these can be said to be providing effective governance either. Poverty, disease, illiteracy, war and environmental problems are eloquent witnesses to a global failure to deliver, and failure to achieve an effective mandate: two basic requirements of good governance.

We have no magic formula to provide effective global governance, although clearly the world needs it. There is no choice but to experiment. Whether they can ever add up to global governance or not, there are some interesting experiments in the environmental field. WWF are responsible for two of the more promising attempts, in the shape of the Marine and Forest Stewardship Councils (MSC and FSC). These organizations bring together businesses with a common interest in maintaining a living resource. Their success has yet to be evaluated but they are undoubtedly making progress. There seem to be several features that are important:

- There is a clear need for action: inter-governmental attempts to maintain fish stocks and to protect forests are demonstrable failures.
- The MSC and FSC captured enough of the players and of the overall resource to create a willingness from NGO and other backers to participate. It is in the interest of players to join the open network that these organizations create.
- They set standards and they have succeeded in getting all three sectors— NGO, commercial and governments—to accept these, albeit incompletely.
- In WWF they had a brand which acted as a trustee of the public good. It

is hard to imagine any company or, indeed, a government achieving such a level of trust.

- They intend to produce labelled products with full traceability in the market place, providing the possibility of consumer agency. (And in the case of the FSC is already successful in this.)

Greenpeace campaigns have worked synergistically with both the MSC and the FSC. We opposed industrial fishing and MSC members left the trade. We campaigned against Canadian clear cuts of ancient forests in British Columbia, and big companies such as Macmillan Bloedell are now making FSC standards their own. Without the FSC it is hard to see how these timber companies would have been able to make the necessary u-turn: it gave them the marketing foundation for a new business case. However, this model will be far more difficult to apply in more complex and messy cases such as energy. While new ways will certainly have to be found at a global level to bring together the three elements of business, governments and NGOs, there is an irreducible role for government itself.

In shaping new forms of global governance the following four principles will need to be applied:

- Companies and governments must accept that there need to be environmentally defined limits. Limits to waste, limits to carbon put into the air, limits to fishing take, limits to forest destruction. Negotiating these limits will inevitably require action by governments. It is hard to see how business can take a leading role in this.
- The social licence for global capitalism or rather anything approaching global free trade, is conditional (and not yet fulfilled). Limits form one of three conditions that are necessary if trade and other economic activity are not to destroy lives, hope and the environment. The three elements are: the move to clean production (continually doing more with less), limits, and standards. At present some of the most progressive businesses have focused on clean production but their trade associations are often fighting limits and standards. That has to stop. There must be globally applied standards to prevent economic activity simply concentrating itself in the place where it can most cheaply abuse the environment (or people). Without limits, for example in the shape of a carbon budget, eco-efficiency does not deliver actual environmental results, only company-wide results.
- Businesses should not try to partition, distribute or own public goods. That is a unique role for government. Businesses will never be trusted in this task as their function is, quite reasonably, to create private wealth. They are simply unsuited to acting as agents of the public as a whole.

And we must now make governments awaken from their post-Keynesian slumber and take up the responsibility so many of them shirk, to design a future for the public, with the public, that can be implemented more directly by the public, than the present arrangement of futile electoral politics coupled with sporadic protest through consumer action.

• And fourth, particularly in rich countries, governments need to accept a new responsibility for investment in public goods: 'social investment' in the widest sense.

As nations get richer in 'real terms' (as New Labour never ceases to tell us we are), two things are happening to the environment. First some of it is eaten up: for example wood, peace and quiet, unpolluted air or water, in order to create the things we count as private 'wealth'. Second, the disposable wealth available to steward and conserve (and consume) public goods is increased. Thus there is both the need and the capacity to do increasingly more, and less and less excuse to degrade or privatize what remains. This simple truth does not yet seem to have lodged in the political mind.

More widely, there is a battle emerging between the promises of post-social democratic democracies such as Britain's and the reality that is delivered. Governments such as Mr Blair's broadly commit citizens to a lower tax burden, and maximize the private, freer enterprise, liberalized global trade and trickle-down benefits. In return we are promised social cohesion, environmental quality (protection of the commons), survival of biodiversity and living resources, and universal education, health rights and international ethics. The trouble is that it does not deliver. The evidence comes from a wide range of issues—patenting of life (including biopiracy), poverty, debt, child rights, underclasses in the 'North', underclass nations, ecological and social refugees, GM food rights and water disputes. We have climate change running at or beyond the 0.2 centigrade per decade that scientists believe will cause (and in the Arctic is already causing) large-scale ecosystem breakdown . We have an AIDS pandemic in Africa. There has been an increase in the number of children orphaned by AIDS of over 400 per cent in three years in seven countries. We have growing, not reducing, inequality within many nations and between the rich and the poor nations. We have a growth in the number of economic and political or conflict-related refugees. According to UNICEF, 16 of 27 developing countries spend more on debt servicing than on basic social services. Together with the continuing destruction of ancient forests and the loss of biodiversity, this is hardly a success for orthodox economics.

We can therefore anticipate the emergence of a new agenda, notable not so much for its content as the coherence of its critique of what has now become conventional economic orthodoxy. The consequent prescription is likely to be little less than a demand to change the logic of the political order, and hence economic priority, away from increasing disposable private wealth, and towards first resourcing basic social services. These include health, education, child development and environmental quality. These will be seen as deserving a first call on investment, along with protection of public goods in the shape of global commons and common environmental heritage, by imposing new limits: physical, technical and moral.

REFERENCES

Anon (1999). *Quality of Life Counts: Indicators for Sustainable Development for the United Kingdom: A Baseline Assessment.* UK Government Statistical Service.

Marr, A. (1995). *Ruling Britannia : The Failure and Future of British Democracy.* London: Michael Joseph.

Stirling, A. (1999). *On Science and Precaution in the Management of Technological Risk.* Brighton: SPRU, University of Sussex.

5

Global Networks and Local Societies:
Cities in the Information Age

Manuel Castells

CITIES are a major source of intellectual creativity and political engagement. We have not finished, and we will never finish, understanding the transformation of cities and the impact of this transformation on society and culture at large. The focus for this chapter is what I would call the great twenty-first century urban paradox—an urban world without cities. Let me try to explain first, and then go into the details of the analysis. I would say that cities have been throughout history sources of cultural creativity, technological innovation, material progress and political democratization. By bringing together people of multicultural origins and by establishing communication channels and systems of cooperation, cities have induced synergy from diversity, dynamic stability from competition, order from chaos. However, with the coming of the information age cities as specific social systems seem to be challenged by the related processes of globalization and informationalization. New communication technologies appear to supersede the functional need for spatial proximity as the basis for economic efficiency and personal interaction. The emergence of a global economy and of global communication systems subdue the local to the global, blurring social meaning and hampering political control traditionally exercised from and by localities. Flows seem to overwhelm places as human interaction increasingly relies on electronic communication networks.

Therefore, cities as specific forms of social organization and cultural expression, materially rooted in spatially concentrated human settlements, could be made obsolete in the new technological environment. Yet, the paradox is that with the coming of the techno-economic system, urbanization—simply understood as spatial concentration—is in fact accelerated. We are reaching a predominantly urban world, which before 2005 will include for the first time in history at least 50 per cent of the planet's population in cities. Core activities and a growing proportion of people are and will be concentrated in multimillion metropolitan regions. This pattern of social–spatial evolution could lead to what I call urbanization without cities. As, on the one hand, people concentrate in spatial settlements, at the same time suburban sprawl defuses people and activities in a very wide metropolitan span. This *may* mean that local societies eventually become socially atomized and culturally meaningless.

Is the culture of cities coming to an end precisely because of the pervasiveness of metropolitan settlements? Are virtual communities and electronically based communication networks, including fast transportation systems, substitutions for the urban community? What are the differential patterns of the spatial concentration and dispersion? How do spatial locality and trans-territorial virtuality interact in the shaping of function, form and meaning? The answer to these questions and therefore the deciphering of these great paradoxes require a long and somewhat complex intellectual detour.

A METROPOLITAN PLANET

Let's start with a few descriptive comments. We are building a metropolitan planet at a fast pace. While our economy and our society are being built on decentralized information networks of interaction powered by the Internet and information technologies, the spatial pattern of human settlement is characterized by an unprecedented territorial concentration of population and activities. In 1970 the urban population accounted for 37 per cent of the total population of the planet. In 1996 the corresponding figure was 46 per cent and we are now about to cross the 50 per cent threshold. Sub-Saharan Africa, the least urbanized region in the world, is in fact the one with the fastest rate of growth: an annual rate of growth over the last 25 years of over 5 per cent. By 2020 63 per cent of sub-Saharan Africans will be likely to live in cities.

At this point South America is about 80 per cent urban. The notion of the South American peasant has become increasingly outdated—perpetuated only by coffee advertising. They in fact exceed the United States who have 78 per cent of the population in urban areas. Western Europe is about 82–83 per cent depending on how you count, Russia is over 75 per cent, Japan and the Korean peninsula are 78 per cent. South East Asia still only reaches about 40 per cent but this is growing fast and the large reserves of rural population are in China and India. China has about 32 per cent of the population being urban and India about 30 per cent—but the projections are staggering, particularly when we count them not only in percentages but also in numbers of people. The most conservative projections from the World Bank lead to a doubling of the Indian urban population between 1996 and 2020, jumping from about 256 million to about 500 million. China's urban population is expected to increase even faster from about 380 million in 1966, to well over 700 million in 2020. Therefore, over half of the projected population growth of China will take place in cities.

This particular process of urbanization takes a metropolitan accent. The percentage of people living in areas of over one million people in Latin America is currently about one third. A similar pattern is true of South Asia. In rich countries towards the end of the twentieth century, about one third of the population were living in these areas of over 1 million people, with the US figure being relatively low at about 27 per cent. Projections are for the increasing concentration of the population in these large metropolitan areas. However, the largest metropolitan settlements in the world are certainly already in the so-called developing world and this will be increasingly the case.

So, we move towards an urbanized world and at the core of this urbanized world a metropolitan world of unprecedented scale and growth. In other words the rate of growth of the largest agglomeration is higher than the rate of the urban agglomeration, which is higher than the rate of growth of the population at large. Does it look like a highly concentrated planet? When people say that there are too many people in the planet, maybe in some respects this is true but in terms of actual occupation of land certainly not, because we have more and more vacant land.

Why is this? Why do urban and metropolitan areas continue to grow in size and complexity in spite of the increasing technological ability to work and interact at a distance? Well, the fundamental and simple answer is an old one that economic geographers know very well. The reason is the spatial concentration of jobs, income-generating activities, services, human development opportunities and leisure activities existing in cities and particularly in the largest metropolitan areas. Why so? Increasing productivity in the advance sector of the economy and the crisis of traditional cultural and constructive activities eliminate jobs in rural areas and layout regions. These processes have induced new rural–urban migrations, as we know. Migrations are on the rise everywhere. The only countries that don't have migrations are those countries that have tactically exhausted their rural population and then they compensate this with international migration. On the other hand, metropolitan areas concentrate high income-generating activities both in manufacturing and services. Studies on the development of cities demonstrate the concentration of creativity, informational productivity and the ability to generate wealth out of ideas in all major cities in the world. Because major and the larger metropolitan areas are sources of wealth they provide jobs both directly and indirectly. And because there is a high level of income in this area they offer greater opportunities for the provision of essential services, such as education and health. Furthermore, even for those migrants at the bottom of the urban society, the spill-over opportunities provide better chances for survival and opportunities for their children in the future than those that could be found in increasingly marginalized rural areas and depressed regions. I would also argue that, as metropolitan areas continue to be cultural centres of innovation, the residents have access to unparalleled chances of cultural enhancement and personal enjoyment.

MILIEUX OF INNOVATION

However, we understand this is true but it is still descriptive. People concentrate in the metropolitan areas because it is where wealth is created and where the greatest opportunities are found. This is not strange. The strange thing would be the opposite. But then we have to answer the following question: why are metropolitan areas, and in particular the largest ones, the centres or the nodes of wealth creation, cultural innovation and informational productivity? Well, precisely because we are in the information age, wealth is created on the basis of knowledge-generation and information-processing. The information age is not just about the Internet. The Internet is the medium and the organizational form through which informational activities proceed, but what is absolutely critical is the power of information technologies to reinforce the role of knowledge-generation and information-processing as sources of value.

Both knowledge-generation and information-processing depend on innovation and then on the capacity to diffuse innovation into networks that induce synergy by sharing its information and knowledge. Here is where I start connecting to some of the research that a number of colleagues and myself have been doing for at least twenty years. A whole tradition of urban and regional research has shown the importance of territorial complexes of innovation-facilitating synergy. Again here in historical terms I refer to the work by Peter Hall (1998). Peter Hall and myself came up with the term 'milieux of innovation' some time ago. It refers to the capacity of territorial complexes of production, information-processing, research and creativity to be at the heart of the ability of cities to be the sources of wealth in the information age. This is in empirical terms certainly the case of Silicon Valley and the San Francisco Bay area at large, as shown in the work by Anna Saxenian (1996), also by the survey that

Peter Hall and myself (1994) did on a number of technopoles around the world, that have now become major centres of technological innovation, all appearing in and from large metropolitan areas in the world. I would say the relationship between cities and innovation extends to the entire western history of cultural creativity and entrepreneurial innovation. If so, it seems logical that when we reach the information age, cultural creativity and intellectual innovation become productive forces, therefore reinforcing cities' competitive advantage as sources of wealth.

This is not only true of information technology industries. It is also, even more so, the case in advanced business services, which are leading money-making sectors in our economy. Services such as finance, insurance, consulting, legal services, accounting and marketing are at the nerve centre of the twenty-first century economy. And they are concentrated in large metropolitan areas and increasingly so. The back offices are decentralized in the middle of nowhere; by and large the advanced services economies are highly metropolitan. In the USA, New York and New Jersey continue to be the prominent areas for these services. Advanced services are also unevenly distributed between the central business district and the new suburban centres depending on the history and the spatial dynamics of each area. In New York, Manhattan still dominates as central London does in London, but in places like Atlanta it is the suburban North Atlanta area which has developed. In Europe in general the historic centre of the city tends to keep the advanced business services sector concentrated there. What is critical in this process is that advanced services centres are territorially concentrated, built on interpersonal networks of decision-making processes and then organized around a territorial web of suppliers and ancillary services which are absolutely vital to these centres.

A third set of value-generating activities, also concentrated in metropolitan areas and also extremely important sources of wealth creation, are cultural industries. There is much more value added from cultural industries these days than from manufacturing in our societies. Media in all forms—entertainment, art, fashion, publishing—are industries that tend to be concentrated territorially in milieux of innovation with a multiplicity of interactions and face-to-face exchanges at the core of the innovation process. This is complemented, not contradicted, by on-line interaction. Moreover, the development of the Internet—the ultimate placeless technology—has led to an increasing concentration of Internet domains. A student of mine, Matthew Such, is finishing his dissertation in Berkeley, having produced among other things the first world map on a representative sample of Internet domains. Surprise, surprise: the Internet content-providers—that is the Internet key industry—is the most concentrated industry of all. The reason for that is even more interesting. It is actually concentrated in very large metropolitan areas, mainly in the older San Francisco Bay area, New York, London and Los Angeles, and within these major areas, within specific localities, and even within these localities in specific neighbourhoods. It is a pattern of increasing spatial concentration of Internet companies. Why? Among other things this is linked to the regionalization of venture capital markets. The most important factor in the development of Internet companies is who provides the money to fulfil your crazy idea. Any crazy idea these days in Silicon Valley starts at $2 million. You decide to sell something on the web, you get $2 million. It's a game of chance. It can be worth hundreds of millions of dollars so it comes down to very good economic calculations. Venture capital firms are not anonymous financiers throughout the world; anonymous financiers subcontract venture capital firms that are linked to a network of territorially concentrated innovators. It is very much like Hollywood with crazy people writing scripts and trying to be stars. In other words, if the milieu of innovation is there then the venture capital firms go into this milieu of innovation, find people who have the ideas and then work with them in the development of the business project. These venture capital markets are highly regionalized so there is as much money in principle in the Chicago Board of Trade as in the San Francisco Bay area. One third of all venture of capital invested in the US is invested in the San Francisco Bay area by venture capital companies themselves located in the San Francisco Bay area. London is a similar story, and so on and so on. Therefore, global flows ultimately land in a few places. The Internet industry although placeless—based on electronic network—will end up where the technological innovation and the business innovation connect with venture capital in regionalized markets.

The last point on this matter relates to why there is metropolitan concentration in the information age. It is precisely because of the existence of advanced telecommunication networks that this milieu of innovation and these high levels of decision-making can exist in a few nodes in the country or in the planet and then connect to the entire world. If the fashion firms or the business services based in Manhattan or the city of London have to maintain a presence everywhere in the planet to be able to manage a global system of production and distribution, then they would have to be spatially distributed. If you have very advanced Internet-based telecommunication systems then you can run the world from a few blocks in a few areas; not just from one place, but from a few nodes on the entire planet.

A GLOBAL GEOGRAPHY OF NETWORKS

This leads me to the third point of the analysis, which is the emergence of a new geography made of networks of metropolitan nodes. The concentration of population in major metropolitan areas occurs because this is where wealth, jobs and opportunities are generated. Now, these metropolitan areas are created as sources of wealth because they are linked to information processes and knowledge generation; because of this they keep increasing the concentration of activities and population. But then they connect to the rest of the world, they are not isolated. In that sense they are the nodes of the process of globalization. Globalization is the process by which the core activities of the economy, of science and technology, and of strategic decision-making are linked world-wide in real time, therefore, having the potential of really working as a unit on a planetary scale. So, in fact most activities are not global; they are local or regional, but the job of these activities and the livelihood of people involved in these activities are largely dependent on a globalized core, on a global network between nodes settled in different areas of the world. Because these core activities are based in major metropolitan areas there is a concomitant process of global interaction between these metropolitan nodes. This process has often been described by the misleading concept of global city, which I proposed some years ago but I think it was widely misunderstood. In this view some cities are global, others are half-global, others are a little global, others are not global. Well, with this kind of urban hierarchy analysis we don't need a new concept; we have an old concept—the urban hierarchy proposed by the French geographers in the 1960s, and we have also the old concept proposed by Friedmann (1986) of world cities to indicate the big stuff, the cities that are really important. If we have to introduce something new it is for some different reason.

The global city is not one particular city, it is a process of linkage and interaction between the globalized cores of many cities. In that sense it is false that London is a global city. London is very global, absolutely global if you look from the city of London or if you look from advanced business services; it is very local if you look from, say, Hampstead. Tokyo is superglobal if you look from the business districts. Kunitachi, for example, is very local and it could not be more remote from the notion of globalization. So, when we say 'global cities' what we are actually meaning is one global city which is trans-territorial, which is made of bits and pieces of cities around the world which connect in a global network of interaction and processing of the core dominant activities of our planet. And then this global city extends to more than places, includes international hotels, includes airports (certain airports), includes fast transportation systems, includes a whole culture and symbolism that goes with the globalization of core dominant activities. In that sense what is critical is to recognize the notion of global networks of core or metropolitan regions as the spatial structure of the dominant activities on our planet.

At the same time that these networks expand and integrate everything that is valuable in this world of dominant activities, they disconnect everything that is not interesting and important. We have at the same time a highly articulated planet shrinking to the size of these networks and a highly disarticulated planet switching off from these networks anything that is devalued or is not valued. You wouldn't say that such cities as central Buffalo in New York or central Cleveland, Ohio are global. They are affected by globality but they are being by-passed by the current processes of development. At the same time, even within the same city you have the process of disconnection and connection. You take the second largest city in the world, São Paulo metropolitan area. Well, those of you who haven't been there in the last twenty years may still believe that Avenida Paulista is the centre of São Paulo. However, Avenida Paulista at this point has been disconnected from the world. What is now the centre is something called Avenida Faria Lima, which houses the headquarters of the major multinational corporations. This area is increasingly connected to the world and disconnected from São Paulo.

So, I would say that rather than global cities what we have is global networks of segregated core dominant areas. But, metropolitan regions exist beyond these core areas. There are millions and millions of people and activities. What is happening is that a new spatial form is emerging—and that is where things become complicated. That is what people misunderstand as the impact of new technologies in disintegrating urban agglomerations. What is happening is that within very large spatial settlements there are emerging what I call 'metropolitan regions'. I use 'metropolitan' in order to avoid the word 'city' with its cultural and political connotations. Also, I call it 'region' to indicate that there is a functional connection between activities scattered in a very vast territory, usually defined in terms of specific labour market, specific consumer market and specific media market. Are you aware that the most operational definition of a market for business is the media market—the distribution of areas between different television networks and radio networks. The media have their markets with very precise delimitation, and this is critical. Why? Because this is where they target advertising, which is what for the moment fundamentally finances the media.

So, this metropolitan region is not just a very large urbanized area. It is also a distinctive spatial form. These are large constellations of people and things in an absolutely chaotic pattern which are hauled together by some notion of labour market, consumer market, etc. Don't think it is just an American phenomenon. I live, not all the time, but most of the time in something called The Bay Area. For the initiated that means San Francisco Bay area, but certainly in America you don't even say San Francisco: it is *the* bay area. So, this bay area, to start with, is not central in San Francisco. San Francisco is not the largest city. The largest city is San Jose with one million people. San Francisco has barely 800,000. But then it is more than that. It is more that seven million people who live in a vast expanse that goes all the way north, south, east for about 100 miles from north to south and 60 miles from San Francisco to the east. All these people work in the same labour market, commute, do all kind of possible things every day. You live in that city and then in your little locality, actually in your home. This is even more pronounced in southern California, which is a vast constellation of places, relatively unified and at the same time not necessarily integrated. All this has no cultural homogeneity and no political agency. No one represents these areas, these areas are constellations of local governments adding to each other, more or less trying to live together and do things together—but in fact it is a constellation of micro units working in a macro system with no rules. Southern California in fact has now extended over Mexico.

So, in the rest of the world we are seeing similar processes through specific cultural and institutional economic arrangements. The largest constellation in the world is being formed right now between Hong Kong, Shenzhen, Canton, Macao and the Pearl River Delta with a population currently of about 60 million people working in, I would say, sporadic interaction. It is part of the same system: they are not all working every day to get in the same system but they cannot live without each other. At this point there are seven million workers in manufacturing industries in the Pearl River Delta working for Hong Kong-based companies processing and exporting throughout the world. And living not in Canton, living really in small towns and formerly small villages of the Pearl River Delta.

In Japan, the Yokohama region has already extended to the Osaka Kobe complex on one side and to Kyoto on the other, so that in 3–4 hours within the transportation framework—which is more or less the commuting time for those people who live in central valley and work in silicon valley, California—you have an extraordinary agglomeration of population activities, technology, capital and crime. Then you have a similar things in the Bangkok metropolitan region, in Jakarta metropolis, in Calcutta, in Bombay , in greater Mexico City, greater Buenos Aires, greater Rio de Janeiro, great Paris, greater Moscow and certainly greater London. All these are major areas, most of which have no clear boundaries, no definite identity beyond the vague images of what used to be their central city. And

I am not even mentioning seven plus million areas such as Lima, Bogota, or Manila which continue to grow.

In Western Europe I think that the other major phenomenon which is connected to the same form of constellation is the building of a dense high-speed train network which is integrating London with Paris, finally, Paris with Lyons and Marseille with northern Italy. Paris, Lille and Brussels link with The Netherlands; Frankfurt and Cologne with the French network, and then from the south, Lisbon, Seville, Madrid, Barcelona and Bilbao link up with the French network. By 2004 you will be able to go from Barcelona to Paris in about four and a half hours and from there to Madrid, and from there Seville and Lisbon. So, along these major axes we are creating mega-regions of people who will do as the Italian professors used to do all their lives, which is live in Milan and Rome and teach all over Italy. This is exactly what is happening with Europe: huge transnational urban constellations are developing, in which notions of culture, identity and politics have little to do with the functional unit that we are creating.

CONSEQUENCES AND CRISES

Now, what happens in these things that we have created—within the urban world of the twenty-first century? Well, several things happen. The first, particularly in the developing world, is an ecological crisis of astronomic proportions. The concentration of population in unequipped mega-areas of this kind is at the source of epidemics, of ecological crises, of natural accidents of all kinds of environmental disasters that could be the equivalent—I'm trying not to be too pessimistic—of the bubonic plague of the Middle Ages. We may smile in our world, but look at African cities and look at the Aids epidemic when you have 10, 20, 25 per cent of the population infected with HIV. Things start to look serious and, as many experts are demonstrating, this is in addition to poverty, lack of public services, and urbanization which takes place without any kind of social and institutional control. The reappearance of all kinds of illnesses in many areas of the world go into this direction. In other words, what we have produced, increasingly, is the imbalance between the local ecosystem and the global ecosystem on the basis of this concentration of processes of growth.

A second major issue which is emerging in addition to the ecological crisis, is the social crisis. In the last two decades there has been unprecedented spatial concentration of wealth and poverty in distinctive spaces. Not only has poverty increased but so too has the general trend of increasing spatial concentration of poverty by countries, by regions, by cities and within cities. This is certainly proceeding along the lines of income and ethnicity and it does not limit itself to the traditional split between cities and suburbs.

Residential areas are increasingly specified in their social characteristics, within cities, within suburbs and within the metropolitan area. The newest and most significant trend all over the world is that the upper- and upper-middle income groups are separating themselves from the city, with the exception of a few cities, in particular European cities. But by and large there is a tremendous emphasis placed on building distinct communities, self-segregated communities. In fact, at this point the spatial index of seg-regated concentration of wealth is currently higher than the index of con-centrated segregation of poverty and ethnic minority populations. In other words the rich are more segregated, except that they are segregated in so-called nice places. Which nice places? Well, it is evident in the construction boom in gated communities in many countries in the world, certainly the United States. The fastest growing real estate segment in California is in gated communities but so it is in Cairo, in Bogota, and in many major cities around the world. The main explicit motivation for this is fear of crime and violence.

The new communication technology and metropolitan transportation systems allow people to stay selectively in touch with certain individuals and groups they want to while disconnecting from the city at large. And the development of this increasingly individualized world—atomized in individual homes and grouped in segregated homogeneous communities both at the top and bottom of the social ladder—is tantamount to breaking an urban contract. The urban social contract was the contract by which citizens from different cultures and with different resources accepted being citizens, that is, part of a shared culture and sets of institutions with conflicts as part of life, but where ultimately there was a common ground. The fragmenting of the city and increase in spatial segregation are maybe undermining our capacity to live together. In that sense, the end of the urban contract may signal the end of the social contract.

Therefore, I have been increasingly interested in watching a process of what I call the reconstruction of the city—the reconstruction of the city as a shared culture. Not a nice culture of everybody loving everybody: no, everybody fighting everybody but fighting in meaningful terms—which is different from ignoring everybody. Alienation is not complete. Alienation is when the other does not exist, when the other is outer, the alien. So, what is happening is that cities are being decomposed in atomized worlds which do not relate to each other. When they group, they group by clusters of self-segregated groups. Some of them build commune sort of systems, others build alarmed settlements.

THE RECONSTRUCTION OF CITIES

The reconstruction of cities is taking place along different processes. First of all we have communities and grassroots movements as elements of the reconstruction of the city. However, it is true that community, grassroots groups are declining overall except in communities of resistance. But empirical studies show that some of these communities are rebuilding themselves in their meaning and in their connection, this time through grassrooted Internet connections. We have a whole development of virtual communities which are at the same time local communities, connecting with each other and reconstructing meaning on the basis of their localities. The emerging phenomenon is of local communities which defend their turf and establish a relationship to the overall meaning of society through electronic connections and Internet interactions. The digital city of Amsterdam is one of the most interesting ones, while in the United States, the Seattle community and action network is another.

The second major process that I have observed in the reconstruction of the inner city includes women's networks, particularly in third-world cities. It is women's networks of all kinds of grassroots organizations, and at the same time women taking control of activities that are critical for their survival and their livelihoods, which are rebuilding, in a more practical—I would say less ideological—way the social fabric of the city. Throughout history women have been the deliverers of urban social services and the ones who have clearly made the city even if they were not able to work. But at this point it is more than that: they are taking on, rebuilding the meaning of the city. For instance, I can think of many of the Brazilian movements by women against urban crime, against violence, and for the protection of their children, which are retaking the city from fear.

The third process of reconstruction concerns institutional reconstruction: the decentralization of government to local level and the involvement of local governments in the process of building regional institutions. This is something that in Britain is proceeding with different pace and different success but which is absolutely critical to fill the gap between the actual functioning units, in terms of the spatial settlements, and the political institutions which rarely represent the variety and diversity of people's interest and citizen participation. In other words, decentralization to local governments and to regional government builds the institutional basis for mediation between global and local by new governance institutions. And there the old notion of planning regains its interest. But I would say there is even something more interesting developing in terms of the reconstruction of meaning, not simply of functionality and political participation but reconstruction of meaning in cities. These large agglomerations, which are our cities of the twenty-first century, are being restructured in terms of meaning through a number of initiatives of which we can have very different examples. The main ones seem to be the following.

The reconstruction of urban centrality proceeds on the basis of a new multinuclear structure: not one centre but many centres. This structure does not necessarily imply hierarchy between centres, but requires the combination of functional and symbolic centrality related to the specific subset of the metropolitan region or to the metropolitan region as a whole.

We are seeing the rise of a new monumentality able to provide symbolic meaning to spatial forms, marking in terms of meaning the metropolitan sprawl. Here important developments are public art, singular architecture—urban design oriented to metropolitan infrastructure: telecommunication towers and artistic bridges. Schools are becoming community building devices linking up the last remnants of the family, that is the last common interests: children. People are reorganizing their connections and their lives around taking joint care of the children. They are also reconstructing meaning through new computerized media networks: Internet websites linked to local communities are very important these days. This reconstruction of the public space in electronic space is not the solution, but is one of the elements in the reconstruction of shared meaning and shared institutions.

The explicit interface between a spatial symbolism, centrality, cultural identity and new spatial flows is often articulated in major cultural institutions, which become the nodes of these physical/virtual interface museums. Museums are becoming markers of cities and at the same time launching platforms for meaningful interaction in the electronic circuit. Everybody is talking about the extraordinary success of the Guggenheim Museum in Bilbao. I think it is interesting how a museum which is a New York museum, with a virtual collection designed by a Californian actor becomes the symbol of Basque identity in the reconstruction of an old industrial city. Well, because the marking of the city showed that this city exists and is on the map, visitors flock in and then people in the city say, 'It's true, we are wonderful, let's go to the centre, let's go to things.' This is stimulated not by local communication but by wonderful Internet connections throughout the world. These days what you have in many museums—for example, the Massachusetts Museum of Contemporary Art in the United States or the International Cultural Centre in Barcelona—are markers of the city and a host of interactive networks of cultural interface throughout the world. So you have at the same time a city, new centrality and the hub of connections to the entire world. With these examples I suggest that if the city in our age has to survive as the source of cultural specificity, it must become a hyper-communicated city;

communicated locally and globally, internally and externally, through a variety of communication channels, symbolic, virtual and physical, by building bridges between these channels.

Hopefully through these reconstructive processes the culture of cities in the information age will emerge—culture that will bring together local identity and global networks to restore the interaction between power and experience, function and meaning, technology and culture.

REFERENCES

Castells, Manuel and Peter Hall (1994) *Technopoles of the World.* London: Routledge.

Friedmann, Jonathan (1986). 'The World City Hypothesis', *Development and Change,* 17: 69–83.

Hall, Peter (1998). *Cities in Civilisation,* London: Weidenfeld & Nicolson.

Saxenian, Anna (1996). *Regional Advantage.* Cambridge, MA: Harvard University Press.

6

Cities, People, Planet

Herbert Girardet

As urban areas become our primary habitat—three-quarters of the human population are expected to become city dwellers by around 2050 (Worldwatch Institute 2000)—it is of key importance to establish whether a sustainable relationship can be established between cities and the planet.

The urgency of this task is only too evident: the size of modern cities in terms of numbers of citizens and physical scale is unprecedented: in 1800 there was only one city of a million people: London. At that time the largest 100 cities in the world had 20 million inhabitants, with each city usually extending to just a few thousand hectares. In 1990 the world's 100 largest cities accommodated 540 million people, of which 220 million people lived in the 20 largest cities, mega-cities of over 10 million people, some extending to hundreds of thousands of hectares. In addition, there were 35 cities of over 5 million and hundreds of over one million people (Satterthwaite 1996).

Urban sprawl is a major concern for environmentalists. It is typical of cities of increasing affluence in which people often prefer the spaciousness of suburbs to denser city centres. Metropolitan New York's population, for instance, has grown only 5 per cent in the last 25 years, yet its surface area has grown by 61 per cent, consuming much forest and farmland in the process. In the USA and Europe, sprawl today is above all else caused by the routine use of the motor car.

Los Angeles is famous for the way it sprawls along its vastly complex freeway system. Ninety per cent of its population drive to work by car and many live in detached houses surrounded by large patches of land. A city of 11 million people, it covers an area three times larger than London which has a population of 7 million. London itself, where semi-detached houses are the norm in the suburbs, is several times larger than Hong Kong which has 6 million inhabitants and where most people live in high rise blocks. Not surprisingly, Hong Kong uses space far more efficiently than either LA or London.

Currently the fastest urban growth in the world is under way in China and this is taking place mainly on the country's precious farmland. With some 10 per cent economic growth per year, China is doubling the number of its cities, from just over 600 to over 1200 by 2010. Some 300 million people are expected to be moving to cities, converting from peasant farming to urban-industrial lifestyles.

Large-scale urbanization is a profoundly resource-demanding process —to build as well as to run cities. As people in countries like China switch from peasant farming to urban lifestyles, their per capita use of fossil fuels, metals, timber, meat and manufactured products increases dramatically, typically by some 50 per cent.

Modern cities are the largest structures ever created by humanity. Vast agglomerations like Tokyo, with over 25 million people, or São Paulo, with some 18 million inhabitants—impossible to imagine before the age of coal, oil, steel, industrial mass production and global trade—are now being taken for granted. These vast horizontal and vertical urban structures are all dependent on a continuous supply of energy—for internal and external transportation systems and, of course, for erecting the steel, concrete and glass structures that could not exist without lifts ceaselessly going up and down. The mega-cities of today depend on mega-infrastructures for their energy, water and food supply.

At the start of the new millennium, cities and their resource use dominate life on earth, increasingly affecting the integrity of the global environment. In the last 100 years, human numbers have grown fourfold, whilst both the world economy and urban populations have gone up about fifteenfold (Worldwatch Institute 1999). Today, half of us are city dwellers, whilst the other, the rural half, increasingly depend on urban markets for their economic survival. Due to world-wide urbanization, closely linked to economic and population growth, resource use is continuing to increase. At the turn of the century, humanity, just one of millions of species, already uses around 50 per cent of nature's entire annual production. How much higher could this figure rise? What will be left of the natural world if demands continue to grow?

An urbanizing, industrializing humanity is rapidly changing the very way in which the 'the web of life' itself functions. Until recently, life on earth consisted of the *geographically scattered interaction* of a myriad of living species, to which local human cultures were intimately connected. Now we are moving to a new reality—an *assembly of urban centres* and their resource demands is coming to dominate all life on earth for the benefit of just one species (cf. Castells, this volume). Humanity increasingly funnels resources from all over the biosphere into cities: they currently take up just 2 per cent of the world's land surface, yet they use over 75 per cent of its resources and discharge similar proportions of waste (Girardet 1999).

Cities are also centres of communication, and new electronic systems have dramatically enhanced that role. Information technologies have given cities a global reach as never before, and particularly in further extending the financial power of urban institutions. The daily money-go-round from Tokyo to London and on to New York and Los Angeles is the most striking example of this. Manuel Castells (1996) points out how a new economy is organized around global networks of capital, management, and information, whose access to technological know-how is at the root of productivity and competitiveness. But will this power ever be exercised with a sense of responsibility appropriate to an *urban age*? If this is the global network society, who controls its ever-growing power?

Developing a sustainable relationship between people and planet in the years to come is one of humanity's greatest challenges for the new millennium. We need to conceptualize how:

- the world's urbanization trends can be brought to a halt;
- cities can maintain an equitable relationship with rural areas;
- urban structures and systems can be designed to function sustainably;
- urban communication systems can benefit sustainable development.

If sustainability is the primary frame of reference for planning urban *spaces, structures and processes,* how will we do things differently in the future?

HISTORICAL CITIES AND RESOURCES

Much of the process of large-scale urbanization started in the UK. London's rapid growth, from one million in 1800 to eight million in 1930 was an unprecedented phenomenon. Before that time there had only ever been a handful of cities with populations of up to a million people: Ancient Rome, Constantinople, Shajahanabad (Old Delhi), Edo (Tokyo's predecessor) and Old Peking. Each of these were capital cities and national centres of culture, crafts and industry. They traded food and timber supplies by land, river and sea, relying on renewable energy like fuel wood, muscle and wind power. Only the relatively recent introduction of fossil fuel-based technologies made possible much larger cities of several million people with a global reach.

Never in history had there been a city of more than one million people not running on coal, oil or gas. London's astonishing growth was powered by fossil fuel technologies pioneered in the industrial revolution: coking coal used for smelting of iron; steam power and its use in production, transport and then electricity generation. Together, these made possible the unprecedented processes of urbanization that are still unfolding even today.

Fossil fuel combustion technology and the use of coke in steel production were revolutionary developments because, until then, metal ores had been smelted in small quantities, using limited available quantities of charcoal. Legions of miners and industrial workers, many displaced from farms, manned the new production centres. In the early nineteenth century, when the use of coke became widespread, it made available large quantities of steel for the first time. This caused a revolution in mining, industrial production, building construction, transport and warfare. The unprecedented access to the Earth's stores of resources, and the vast range of new industrial products made in Europe and America, brought about a new prosperity for many, but also profoundly changed the way we inhabit this planet.

By the 1850s, London, by then the largest city ever, numbering some 4 million people, had an increasingly global reach. In his book *The Coal Question*, John Jeavons wrote:

The plains of North America and Russia are our cornfields; Chicago and Odessa our granaries; Canada and the Baltic are our timber forests; Australasia contains our sheep farms; and in Argentina and on the western prairies of North America are our herds of oxen; Peru sends her silver, and the gold of South Africa and Australia flows to London; the Hindus and the Chinese grow tea for us. And our coffee, sugar and spice plantations are all in the Indies. Spain and France are our vineyards and in the Mediterranean are our fruit gardens, and our cotton grounds, which for so long have occupied the Southern United States, are now being extended everywhere in the warm regions of the Earth.

Economic globalization, much talked about in the early twenty-first century, actually made its debut in the mid–nineteenth century. The prolific use of imported resources caused its own local problems. London had to learn to deal with the effects of its extravagant use of resources. It faced three major types of pollution: smog from a million coal fires, soil and water contamination from industrial activity, and the accumulation of ever-growing quantities of human excreta. The latter was particularly acute: seepage of sewage into the groundwater table and its discharge into its rivers caused cholera and typhoid outbreaks, as well as intolerable environmental conditions. 1858 was the year of the 'big stink'—the Thames was so polluted with sewage that the appalling smells halted the debates in the House of Parliament for days on end. Something had to be done: how could London deal with the sewage of so many people?

Various schemes were discussed. One was a circular recycling system, designed like the spokes of a wheel, where the sewage would be flushed to the edge of the city, to be collected and turned into fertiliser for the fields surrounding London. Justus Liebig, then the world's most famous chemist, was called in from Germany to advise the UK government, and he favoured such a scheme. Whilst most people were concerned about the stench in the Thames and the health dangers of sewage contaminating drinking water supplies, Liebig was preoccupied with the loss of plant nutrients from farmland feeding London, as urban sewage was flushed into the sea. Having studied the environmental history of ancient Rome, he argued that it had imported the fertility of North African fields for 200 years as it shipped some 500,000 tonnes of grain to Rome every year. The excreta of a million Romans was then flushed through the *cloaca maxima* into the Mediterranean. In a letter to prime minister Sir Robert Peel he wrote:

The cause of the exhaustion of the soil, is sought in the customs and habits of the towns people, i.e., in the construction of water closets, which do not admit of a collection and preservation of the liquid and solid excrement. They do not return in Britain to the fields, but are carried by the rivers into the sea. The equilibrium in the fertility of the soil is destroyed by this incessant removal of phosphates and can only be restored by an equivalent supply.... If it was possible to bring back to the fields of Scotland and England all those phosphates which have been carried to the sea in the last 50 years, the crops would increase to double the quantity of former years.

Liebig asked himself the question: if many of Europe's cities were to grow like London, and their sewage was not returned to the land, their food demands would rapidly deplete the fertility of farmland feeding them. When London decided to build two massive pipelines and to flush the sewage into the Thames estuary rather than recycle it, Liebig responded by starting work on developing artificial fertilizers. In his view this was the only way for keeping productive farmland feeding cities. These decisions, taken in the nineteenth century, still have a profound effect around the world. Most of the world's cities have built sewage *disposal* rather than *recycling* systems and the farmland feeding cities is being kept productive artificially by the use of chemical fertilizers. But the consequences are there for all to see: today rivers and coastal waters everywhere carry the twin burden of urban sewage and industrial pollutants, as well as the fertilizer and pesticide run-off from farmland feeding cities. But *out of sight* has always been *out of mind*.

On British farms in the nineteenth century, guano from Chile and Peru became the primary source of fertilizer until artificial fertilizers, containing phosphates, nitrates and potash, had been fully developed. Meanwhile the abolition of the corn laws in Britain meant that food, and particularly grain, was increasingly imported from places like Canada and the USA rather than grown at home. When refrigerated ships became available, even meat was imported long-distance from places like New Zealand. A globalizing system for feeding cities got under way.

MODERN CITIES AND RESOURCES

In a world of cities it is crucial to take a new look at the way urban systems function, where their resources come from, and where their wastes end up—in the atmosphere, in rubbish dumps or, indeed, in the rivers and coastal waters. It is essential to find ways to minimize urban impacts on forests, farmland, and aquatic environments as well as the atmosphere. How can we reduce the urban intake of vast quantities of natural resources and the huge output of waste materials? Plausible methods for creating a sustainable relationship between cities and the global environment are urgently required.

Take the water supply to a city such as London. It used to be pumped up from ample supplies in the groundwater table underneath London itself, but 150 years or so of economic activity there resulted in accumulations in the soil of heavy metals or chemicals from gasworks and factories. This made the use of groundwater for drinking purposes increasingly problematic. London is lucky in having another water supply close at hand in the form of the river Thames. However, other cities are not so lucky. Urbanization in dry locations around the world has meant drawing vast quantities of water from large dams constructed in distant rivers. Los Angeles pipes water in from the Colorado and other rivers hundreds of miles away. In China and India, where urbanization is occurring at breakneck speed, vast dams are under construction to meet the water (and electricity) needs of rapidly growing cities. Local rural populations are often deprived of water, as distant cities grow. Similar stories can be told from many parts of the world.

Demand for energy defines modern cities more than any other factor. Yet, most city people have a very limited understanding of the origin of their energy supplies. Our ancestors had the daily task of assuring firewood supplies, but we get electric or gas appliances with the simple flick of a switch. We are hardly aware of the power station, refinery or gas field that our homes are plugged into. Few of us reflect on the environmental impacts of our daily energy use, unless we choke on exhaust fumes on a busy *local* street. But we rarely confront the fact that there is a *global* price to pay: that most of the increase in carbon dioxide in the atmosphere is attributable to combustion within or on behalf of our cities. Ironically some of the primary effects of global warming—rising sea levels—will take a heavy toll on cities: a large proportion are located on low ground close to seashores.

Global urban food supplies are another case in point. Most of us are used to harvesting at the supermarket and we expect food to be served up packaged and branded for enhanced recognition. Yet we are hardly aware of the origins of that food and the impact of food production on the fertility of farmland or the energy required to produce, process and transport it to our homes. An ever-increasing proportion of the fruit and vegetables we eat are flown in by jumbo jet. There are major costs to be considered that are not included in the price. By the time a fruit such as mango, flown in to London from East Africa, arrives on the kitchen table in London, it will have consumed up to 600 times as much energy as it actually contains in calorific value. Many other foods we eat will have required ten to several hundred times as much energy as the food itself actually contains. Yet the environmental cost of the food we eat is simply not reflected in the price we pay in the supermarket.

We can argue that we no longer live in a *civilization*. We live in a *mobilization*—of people, resources and products. Most of the world's transport routes start and end in cities. Their transport-dependent consumption patterns define human global environmental impacts more than any other single factor. Are more and more motorways and airports really needed? Can we make our urban systems less dependent on these transport routes? Should ever more global trade be curtailed for the sake of sustainable development?

A few years ago I spent some weeks estimating the *ecological footprint* of London. The footprint concept originates from the work of Canadian ecologist William Rees. He focused on the three categories: the areas required to *feed* a city; to supply its *timber and paper* needs; and the surface area that would be needed to *reabsorb its* CO_2 output by areas of growing vegetation. If you put these three areas together, London has an ecological footprint the size of the United Kingdom—about 125 times larger than London itself—yet London only has 12 per cent of the UK's population (Girardet 1999). In reality, of course, London's footprint is scattered all over the world.

William Rees and his co-researchers suggested that if other countries adopted the consumption patterns we take for granted in urbanized Europe and in North America, we would need three planets rather than the one we actually live on (Rees and Wackernagel 1992). So, for the rest of the world to copy western lifestyles, requiring something like 3 hectares per person—rather than the 1.5 hectares of productive land actually available per head of the world's population—would be an unrealistic proposition. As the world industrializes and urbanizes, a growing mismatch emerges between human demand patterns and the capacity of the planet to supply. So, we need to find ways to reorganize our urban, economic and technical systems. This requires major changes in tax and subsidy regimes, in the technical use of resources as well as in the administration of our cities.

IMPACTS OF URBANIZATION

I got interested in urban sustainability above all else because I was interested in forests. I came to realize that forests all around the world are disappearing into cities, or are being replaced by cropland to produce animal fodder, or indeed cattle ranches, to supply urban meat demands. And together with the destruction of forests, great damage is also done to the forest cultures that are a most ancient part of our cultural inheritance (cf. Posey, this volume).

Despite many of us seeing TV programmes about the vast, deliberate forest fires set in rainforest areas like the Amazon, Malaysia and Indonesia, we don't often make the connection to our daily urban lives. Yet, as cities grow and increase their demands, forests recede, and with them their plant, animal and human populations. All too often these forests are not replanted. In any case, virgin rainforests and their unique assembly of species cannot be replaced once they are burned or cut down. Temperate timber forests in places like Sweden, Canada or Siberia *are* being replanted, but their original biodiversity is greatly depleted.

In Mato Grosso on the southern edge of the Amazon, major impacts on savannah and forest are now occurring. Forests there are being cleared on a vast scale to create farmland for producing and exporting soybeans to Rotterdam, Tokyo, and increasingly Shanghai or Beijing, to meet the growing demand for meat that results from increased affluence. Feedlot cattle, pigs and chicken in Asia and Europe are increasingly fed on soybeans from Brazil's rainforest areas. Wherever disposable income grows, meat consumption also rises. So, we are seeing the ever-larger *ecological footprints* of our cities across the world. Trading systems based on ever more sophisticated transport and communication technologies make it possible for these global links to be established (Juma, this volume).

The impact of cities is not solely terrestrial. The earth's atmosphere has become the sink for their waste gases, with dire consequences. Since the beginning of the industrial revolution CO_2 in the atmosphere has increased by some 30 per cent. Global climate change is becoming an irrefutable reality, and related to it the ever-growing incidence of storms, floods and irregular weather patterns. All in all, the environmental impacts generated by global urbanization need to be met with a wide range of creative responses.

Is worldwide urbanization inevitably a road to global environmental destruction? Or can we transform cities into much less environmentally demanding and damaging places than they are today? Is it possible to redesign urban systems to assure a sustainable relationship between urbanized people and the planet?

Given the vast environmental impacts of urbanization today, cities would be well advised to remodel their functioning by mimicking natural ecosystems. These are generally systems of permanence, whereas currently man-made systems, such as cities, are characterized by high levels of entropy. Natural systems like forests or coral reefs function quite differently. All their waste materials are beneficially reabsorbed into their living fabric, contributing to the long-term viability of the whole system. If we want sustainable cities in the future, we had better study carefully how natural eco-systems seem to be able to exist indefinitely, powered only by sunlight.

RETHINKING URBAN METABOLISMS

In recent years I have had the opportunity to study the metabolism of London, quantifying the resources that go into this city and the wastes that come out the other end. The metabolism of cities like London, now a city of seven million people, is basically linear—resources are taken from somewhere, and the biosphere is used as a sink for their wastes. Every year 14 million tonnes of non-biodegradable solid waste are dumped in holes in the ground, such as Mucking in Essex, which will take thousands of years to break down.

Whilst many cities today have a *linear* metabolism, nature's own ecosystems have an essentially *circular* metabolism. Every output by an individual organism is also an input that renews the whole living environment of which it is a part: the web of life hangs together in a chain of *mutual benefit*. To become sustainable, cities have to develop a similar circular metabolism, using and re-using resources as efficiently as possible and minimizing materials use and waste discharges into the natural environment.

The concept of the city as a dynamic and ever-evolving *super-organism* helps us formulate strategies for a sustainable urban future. New communication systems and computer modelling can help us *reinvent* the city

(Castells, this volume). In this context individuals and communities should have an important role in decision-making. Sustainability implies cybernetic feedback systems that help us to continually adjust our relationships to each other and to the outside world.

Change will occur at different levels and scales of impact, ranging from individual action, community interaction and government policy. *Thinking* comprehensively about our cities is an important starting point in the process of remodelling them. To rethink the city, we must first accept its complexity, and the myriad of interrelationships that define it. The real challenge, however, is to *act* differently. As we start working towards evolving a more beneficial interaction with natural systems, a profound impact on their appearance and working will occur. It is quite apparent now that there can be no sustainable development without sustainable *urban* development. In a world of cities, suitable policies for transforming the way cities work are a key issue. This is recognized both in key UN documents such as Agenda 21, drawn up at the Rio UN Earth Summit in 1992, and in the Habitat Agenda, signed by the world's nations at the UN City Summit in Istanbul in 1996.

It could be argued that it makes environmental sense for people to congregate in cities. They have the potential for great resource efficiency through closed-loop economies, diversity and mutuality. Economic well-being need not automatically mean growth in the consumption of resources. Sustainable development requires new technical and organizational solutions to ensure the efficient use of resources, minimizing pollution and waste. It is increasingly apparent that this can also have great social and economic benefits: new renewable energy systems, for instance, can supplant fossil fuel supplies from outside cities, creating many new local jobs.

So what is a sustainable city? I use the following definition: *A 'sustainable city' enables all its citizens to meet their own needs and to enhance their well-being without damaging the natural world or endangering the living conditions of other people, now or in the future.*

To implement sustainable urban development, circular and highly productive systems need to be put in place, making efficient use of resource as well as the land surfaces. Among other things this means reduced distances between resources supply and demand: sustainability requires us to re-introduce the concept of *proximity* in order to help increase the efficiency of urban consumption patterns—even if this flies in the face of the gospel of competitive advantage. For instance, could at least some of the food we consume in our cities come from urban regions?

The growth of urban agriculture is a significant trend in cities all over the world, rich and poor. In Havana, Cuba, for instance, as a result of the collapse of the Soviet Union and the loss of sugar sales to Russia, an economic emergency arose. The city authorities in Havana dealt with it very creatively. Using compost made from bagasse, a waste product of the sugar cane industry, they created so called 'organoponicos', a cultivation system based on raised beds extending right within the city itself. Havana is a spacious city and people there could utilize tens of thousands of acres to grow a wide range of vegetables and fruit. The new gardens permeate the city and the gardeners market their produce from their own cooperative shops.

Shanghai, too, used to be permeated with vegetable gardens but its rapid growth has reduced the farmland available within the city. 'Intra-urban' agriculture has been replaced by 'peri-urban' agriculture in recent years: urban farming is being transferred to the edge of the city. Shanghai's city authorities administer a total of 600,000 hectares of land, half of which is built-up areas whilst the other half is farmland used for supplying a large proportion of the city's food needs. Similar systems operate in many other Chinese cities. This is a very cost-effective and energy-efficient urban food system that the Chinese authorities have no intention of giving up. In Shanghai alone it employs 270,000 people out of a total population of 13 million.

Urban agriculture is not just a phenomenon of developing countries either. In the Bronx, New York, vegetable gardens are thriving in the poorer communities and the same applies to other cities across the USA. Peri-urban agriculture is expanding fast. In the last decade over 4000 new farmers' markets have been created in American cities, mainly supplied by peri-urban growers, as more and more consumers are attracted to eating food bought from local farmers they actually know.

Across the world there are many initiatives under way to localize supplies and to create circular and resource-efficient urban systems. Recycling of steel and aluminium, for instance, reduces some of the need for mining virgin ores. The same is true for paper. In the US in recent years pulp mills tend to be built near cities, rather than near forests, because cities can supply huge quantities of waste paper, reducing the need for using trees for making paper.

Many of these developments are market-driven, yet they can be further accelerated by government policy. For instance, shifting taxes from labour to resources can help turn a wasteful 'disposal society' into one that practises reuse and recycling. In Britain in 1995, the 'landfill tax' was introduced, making it more expensive to dump waste in holes in the ground. As a result, the behaviour patterns of companies are changing, encouraging new recycling initiatives. Take UK road construction companies: until recently they took gravel extraction for road building for granted. Higher disposal costs because of the landfill tax made them think again. Now it is becoming economic when renewing roads to scrape up old road surfaces and recycle them: a much more sustainable use of hardcore.

At present in the UK only 8 per cent of household waste is recycled. Meanwhile the European Union insists on ever-higher recycling rates. Across continental Europe, 40 per cent is the norm and rising. In the US, too, 30 to 35 per cent is now taken for granted. In Europe or the USA we are in the habit of using capital-intensive methods for recycling waste. In third-world cities even higher recycling rates are often achieved than in Europe or the US. Most waste materials end up being reused, recycled and remanufactured. Waste collectors are much in evidence, pushing their carts through the streets and using labour-intensive methods for waste recycling.

Some third-world cities have implemented innovative waste management policies. In the southern Brazilian city of Curitiba, the city authorities found it more cost-effective and socially beneficial in the narrow streets of poorer districts to involve communities in waste collection and recycling than sending in heavy waste trucks. People in the 'favellas' collect and separate their own rubbish and deliver it to key collection points twice a week, where it is exchanged for fresh vegetables, grown on city compost. Thus people participate not only in cleaning up their neighbourhoods, but also consume healthy food supplied free of charge by the city authorities. Overall, this system is more efficient than the use of heavy trucks to collect and dump waste in holes in the ground.

Alternative approaches to sewage treatments are also gaining ground around the world. Recently Wessex Water in Bristol decided to dry the city's entire sewage output, to pellet it and convert it into small granules, called Biogran. This is sold to farmers as soil conditioner and fertilizer. The former slag heaps in Merthyr Tydfil in South Wales, which were eyesores after the coal mines there were closed down, have been 'regreened' using Bristol's dried, pelleted sewage. Instead of dumping sewage in the sea, a circular system for reusing urban sewage has been implemented. This system is not without problems: it only captures some of the nitrates and phosphates contained in sewage, and the pellets can contain trace quantities of heavy metals. However, a useful start has been made in upgrading sewage technology.

A critical issue for the future is whether urban systems that have been created by the use of fossil fuels (and nuclear power) could run on renewable energy technology instead. Until the 1960s, cities such as London trucked in coal from outside the city to be burned in stoves and local power stations. The resulting smog caused major health problems. As a result of the Clean Air Act, passed in the early 1960s, power stations were relocated hundreds of miles away from cities, discharging their smoke plumes from tall chimney stacks. This solved local air pollution problems in cities, but caused major acid rain problems downwind instead. It is also a very inefficient use of fossil fuels because only 30 per cent of the actual energy contained in the coal or the gas is actually converted into electricity. But today we have realistic alternatives.

Greater energy efficiency in supplying power to our cities and greater efficiency in urban energy consumption, together, are preconditions for improving urban energy performance. It is crucial to find ways to implement non-polluting energy alternatives within cities themselves. Can we create more sustainable, more local, renewable energy systems for our cities?

ALTERNATIVES

Many alternative options can be cited. At Smithfield Market, in London, a former cold store has been turned into a *combined heat and power* (CHP) *station* which now supplies electricity to the grid. It operates at 90 per cent efficiency with virtually no acid gases coming out of the high-technology chimney, making much better, more efficient use of fossil fuels by producing electricity as well as hot and chilled water for local use. Such CHP systems are a rarity in the UK but they are commonplace in most cities in Scandinavia, greatly reducing per-capita energy consumption. Today the annual CO_2 output of a Stockholm citizen, at five tonnes per year, is half the figure for a Londoner.

An even more important new energy technology is photovoltaic (pv) cells. Until a few years ago they were only used in calculators or satellites. Photovoltaic electricity is still four to five times more expensive than conventional, but the cost is expected to come down rapidly in the next few years due to rapidly increasing demand and increasingly automated production of pv cells. Large-scale government support programmes in Japan, Europe and America now give households and companies substantial financial incentives to install pv cells on the roofs and walls of buildings. As a result, a boom in the use of photovoltaics is now underway. Housing estates, sports stadiums and public buildings are now being fitted with pv panels to help them become largely self-sufficient in electricity. According to research by PB Solar, even cloudy cities such as London could be largely self-sufficient in electricity from available surfaces covered in PV panels.

Fuel-cell technology has started another energy revolution. This highly efficient technology converts hydrogen straight into electricity without combustion, using an electro-chemical process. Fuel cell-powered buses, trucks and cars are expected to be mass-produced within a few years. One important advantage they have for cities is that they don't burn fuel when they are stationary in traffic jams or in front of traffic lights. Fuel cells can also be used for powering boats, buildings and whole urban districts. In various cities in Europe and America, fuel-cell power stations are now coming on stream, making very efficient use of pure hydrogen, as well as natural gas or methanol.

It is clear that the energy systems powering our cities can be dramatically improved and their dependence on fossil fuels greatly reduced. London is a case in point. It currently consumes around 20 million tonnes of oil equivalent every year and discharges about 60 million tonnes of CO_2. By the introduction of a combination of energy efficiency, combined heat and power and photovoltaic and fuel-cell technology, that figure could be halved in the coming decades. There is also a huge job creation and business potential. Tens of thousands of new jobs would be created by *re-localizing* the energy systems of a city such as London. But for sustainable urban energy systems to be created, it is vital for appropriate government and local authority policies to be implemented.

Integrated transport for cities is another case in point. This is often talked about, but good examples are hard to find. Here, again, the city of Curitiba in Brazil has taken significant policy initiatives. Growing rapidly to 1.6 million people over thirty years, the city set about organizing a very efficient and highly integrated bus system to service the entire city, making it pleasant and fast to move around without the huge expense of constructing an underground system. Curitiba created a hierarchy of bus services— from ones only serving local neighbourhoods to fast, articulated buses that run across the city on dedicated routes. By replacing conventional bus stops with so-called loading tubes, bus travel is greatly speeded up: as people enter the tubes they pay the resident conductor and when the bus arrives, everyone can get on and off instantly.

But as important as creating integrated transport systems is the creation of local lifestyles that don't require motorized transport in the first place. In Holland and elsewhere on the European continent cycling is taken for granted in many cities, and lifestyles are organized around *short journeys* wherever possible. Pedestrianization is another case in point and is being widely implemented. The muscle power that enables us to ride bikes or walk originates from food and drink. What a simple, practical way of powering sustainable urban transport.

CONCLUSION

Part of the problem of our cities at present is that that they are perceived by many people as inhospitable places that they want to get away from, given half a chance. Many people dream of the green and pleasant land on the edge of the city and beyond, where they think they can get closer to nature and, maybe, get more peace of mind. This is a great challenge for urban planning. It is crucial that we learn to recreate cities as places that are sedentary, which are not centres of *mobilization* but centres of *civilization* again, of urban culture and of the urbane, creative interchange between people.

It is vitally important to find ways to turn our cities into truly hospitable, convivial places, with a wide range of community facilities, meeting places, piazzas, parks and neighbourhood gardens. We need to create conditions in which people can develop a pride of place, truly enjoying their daily urban lives. That also means improving the architecture of our cities, getting away from the repetitive right angles and straight lines that characterize so many recent buildings. We should create buildings with solar façades that are highly energy-efficient; but they should also be beautiful, imaginative and even a bit eccentric. Many cities have some unusual recent buildings, such as Gaudi's creations in Barcelona, or Hundertwasser's buildings in Vienna, that have proved to be highly popular with locals and also with visitors. Modern cities greatly benefit from such non-standard building design, greatly enlivening the urban ambience.

There is enormous pent-up creativity present in all cities. Techniques such as neighbourhood forums, consensus building and action planning should be widely used to liberate this creativity because it invariably leads to improved social interaction. The active dialogue between city people about shared concerns strengthens democratic processes and widens people's horizons. This is crucial since I believe that there can be *no sustainability without participation.* We need to develop new *cultural feedback* mechanisms, enabling city people to learn about environmental conditions and impacts, or about new 'best practice' examples of sustainable development that may be relevant to their cities.

We can do much to change the way we design and run our cities. Many people are becoming increasingly aware that efforts to improve the living environment must focus on cities and urban lifestyles. Cities the world over cannot avoid participating in a globalizing economy, but we can, nevertheless, help create urban systems that are highly resource efficient and less dependent on unsustainable global supplies. Eco-friendly, more self-reliant urban development is one of the greatest challenges of the twenty-first century. The tools for this are policy, technology and participation.

I am, of course, aware of the many other problems facing cities at the turn of the new millennium: deep social inequalities, grinding poverty and squatter-camp living for millions, homelessness, unemployment and intra-urban water, air and soil pollution (see Girardet 1992, 1996). These problems are particularly acute in the fast-growing cities in developing countries. Much effort has gone into trying to address them through numerous initiatives at local, national and global level.

In this chapter I have focused primarily on the issue of the environmental sustainability of cities, or the current lack of it—because this urgent issue is often overlooked in the debate about the future of cities. In a world of cities much needs to be done to understand better that there cannot be *sustainable* development without *sustainable urban* development.

REFERENCES

Castells, M. (1996). *The Network Society*. Oxford: Blackwell.

Girardet, H. (1992, 1996). *The Gaia Atlas of Cities: New Directions of Sustainable Urban Living*. London: Gaia Books.

Girardet, H. (1999). *Creating Sustainable Cities*. Dartington: Green Books.

Rees, W. and M. Wackernagel (1992). *Our Ecological Footprint*. Gabriola Island, BC: New Society Publishers.

Satterthwaite, D. (1996). *An Urbanizing World: The Second Global Report on Human Settlements*. Oxford: Oxford University Press.

Worldwatch Institute (1999). *State of the World 1999*. Washington, DC.

Worldwatch Institute (2000). *State of the World 2000*. Washington, DC.

7

Global Sustainable Development

Maurice Strong

To environmentalists the concept of *globalism* is not new. Indeed the environmental movement is based on the realization that the environment and natural resources of the earth, which nourish and sustain life on our planet, are systemic in nature and intrinsically global in scale. Thus environmentalists tend to perceive even the most local of conditions as being linked to the complex system of cause and effect relationships on which the health of the environment of our planet as a whole depends. The processes through which human activity impacts on, and interacts with, this global system have accelerated to an unprecedented degree during the past century through the phenomenon we now call *globalization*. This can be seen by environmentalists as a mixed blessing. On one hand, it has vastly increased public awareness of the global nature of environmental issues and provided the impetus for international actions to deal with them. On the other hand, globalization has been driven largely by economic motivations which have served to accelerate the environmental deterioration that we have witnessed during this last century, particularly the latter part of it, and which continue to undermine the earth's natural capital.

Knowledge is clearly the principal resource on which the future growth, development and governance of our civilization will be based. Technology manifested in a galaxy of new products and services, design, management and information systems is the primary source of added value and comparative advantage in the global economy (Castells, this volume). It also offers the main ingredient for the transition to sustainability through patterns of production and consumption that are less physical in nature, and less materials- and energy-intensive. The value of a compact disk or a computer chip is primarily attributable to the functions and characteristics with which human intelligence and technology have endowed it, rather than to its material content. This dematerialization of economic growth is already evident in the fact that the biggest single export of the United States today, amounting to some $30 billion per year, is entertainment. The dematerialization of our economic life provides the most promising pathway to a sustainable future.

The unparalleled advances in science and technology that have driven the processes of globalization have created a series of imbalances and inequities, which threaten the very viability of our civilization. Extremes of poverty and wealth divide the beneficiaries from the victims of globalization. Ours is the wealthiest civilization ever, with unprecedented capacity for creation of still more wealth. Thus the existence of pervasive poverty in a world which has the capacity to eradicate it must be seen as an affront to the very moral basis of our civilization and a threat to its sustainability.

Over the past decades the income gap between the richest fifth of the world's population and its poorest fifth has more than doubled to some 74 to 1. The same processes have also produced a plethora of new knowledge and new tools to help us understand and manage their impacts. There is no more dramatic example than the unprecedented growth of the Internet, which had 140 million users in 1998, and was estimated to exceed 700 million by 2001.

But this phenomenal increase in our capacity to manage has not been matched by an increase in the will to do so. My main thesis, then, is that the prospects for the global environment in the new millennium now depend primarily on our motivations and our will to use the knowledge and capacities we now have to manage the transition to a sustainable future. Implementation depends on motivation, and motivation must now become our priority. It is in this context that I would like to review briefly how we got to this point.

PRECURSORS OF THE ENVIRONMENT AND SUSTAINABLE DEVELOPMENT MOVEMENT

For centuries the dominant attitude towards the natural world was that it existed for the benefit of humankind, to exploit as we saw fit. 'The world is made for man, not man for the world,' Francis Bacon wrote some 400 years ago. This remained the dominant attitude of people towards nature until recent times, and still today conditions the attitudes of many. But in the nineteenth century the negative impacts of the industrial revolution and the increased urbanization which arose from it led to the development of a number of voluntary associations. These were the precursors of the conservation movement and the broader concepts of environment and sustainable development which evolved from it. England was home to one of the first of these: the Commons, Open Spaces and Footpath Preservation Society, established in 1865. In 1888 the Fog and Smoke Committee was created to press for improvement of urban air quality. In America, Henry David Thoreau dramatized the damaging effects on the human spirit, and on nature, of the encroachment of industrial and urban life into the wilderness areas of New England. George Perkins Marsh of Vermont in his monumental book, *Man and Nature; or, Physical Geography as Modified by Human Action* (1864), documented the systematic and pervasive impact of human activity on nature and how it reverberated to undermine human welfare.

The insight that humans inflict damage on themselves by damaging nature has become a basic premise of modern environmentalism as it emerged as a major and influential movement during the second half of the twentieth century. Impacts of air and water pollution, urban blight, desecration of natural resources and undermining of human health and well-being have became more widespread and visible. The impacts were dramatically pointed out by Rachel Carson in her influential book, *Silent Spring* (1964). The dire predictions of the Club of Rome's *Limits to Growth* (Meadows 1972) did not prove accurate in all respects, but did call attention to the systemic and pervasive nature of the phenomenon.

These all helped to foster growing public awareness and concern in industrialized countries, which led to the decision by the United Nations General Assembly, on the initiative of Sweden, to hold the United Nations Conference on the Human Environment. The Conference was held in Stockholm in June 1972, the first of the major conferences that have done so much to shape the agenda of the United Nations (UN) and the world community during the three decades that followed. It placed the environmental issue firmly on the global agenda and provided the political impetus which led to the convening of several other global conferences on related issues, such as on population in Bucharest in 1974 and Cairo in 1994. I will not name them all, but they also led to the development of environmental ministries or their equivalent agencies in most countries— very few had them prior to Stockholm.

Each of the conferences that followed was patterned on the model pioneered by the Stockholm Conference, most notably in providing for substantial participation on the part of civil society organizations. The environment issue and the more comprehensive issue of sustainable development which evolved from it provide a broad framework in which economic, social, population, gender and human settlements issues can be seen in their systemic relationship with each other. They provide the common thread that links the agendas and the results of each of these conferences. In this sense, Stockholm was their logical precursor.

The Stockholm Conference then led to a proliferation of new environmental initiatives and the creation of the United Nations Environment

Programme (UNEP), headquartered in Nairobi, Kenya. But despite progress in many areas it became evident by the mid-1980s that overall the environment was deteriorating, while the population and economic growth largely responsible for this was continuing. In response, the United Nations General Assembly established a World Commission for Environment and Development under the chairmanship of Norway's Gro Harlem Brundtland (1987). Its report, *Our Common Future*, made the case for sustainable development as the only viable pathway to a secure future for the human community. Its recommendations led to the decision by the UN General Assembly in December 1989 to hold a UN Conference on Environment and Development (UNCED). The Assembly agreed to hold it in a developing country, Brazil, and specifically Rio de Janeiro. To underscore the importance of the Conference, it was decided that it should be held at the 'summit level' (meaning that delegations would be led by heads of state), and it is now known universally as the Earth Summit.

THE EARTH SUMMIT

As an event in itself, the Earth Summit was clearly remarkable, perhaps even historic. Never before had so many of the world's political leaders come together in one place, and the fact that they came to consider the urgent question of our planet's future put these issues under an enormous spotlight. We arranged that I would have them for one hour without assistants, without support staff, without ministers, in a room—just the leaders and myself and Boutros-Ghali, who was then the Secretary General. During that hour I had the sense that they really accepted the premise that the issues that they had come to Rio to address were literally more important for the future of their people than most of the things that were actually preoccupying their own particular national agendas at the time. Unfortunately, that impression did not endure, but it did seem to be manifest during that hour.

The whole spirit of the Conference was very much helped and lifted by the non-governmental organization (NGO) presence, which was massive —an unprecedented number of non-governmental representatives, including many that were not part of the normal NGO circuit. We made a point of getting the NGOs from the developing world, including those who were not accredited to the UN. Most of the developing countries' NGOs were not registered with the UN because they did not have the capacity or the resources to do that, so we invited them all. We made relevance the key criteria for UNCED accreditation and we got unprecedented numbers. It was extremely important to setting the spirit that infected the official conference. I am quite sure that the conference would not have had even the results that it did without the presence of that dynamic and motley group of non-governmental representatives.

The Earth Summit validated the concept of sustainable development which had been articulated by the Brundtland Commission, not as an end in itself but as the indispensable means of achieving in the twenty-first century a civilization that is sustainable in economic and social, as well as in environmental, terms. The economist Herman Daly summed up well the conditions that would have to be met in this transition to achieve physical sustainability. 'The rates of renewable resources should not exceed the rates of regeneration. The rates of use of non-renewable resources should not exceed the rate at which sustainable renewable substitutes are developed. The rates of pollution emission should not exceed the assimilative capacities of the environment.' But the Earth Summit also made clear that sustainability in physical terms can only be achieved through new dimensions of cooperation amongst the nations and peoples of our planet, and most of all through a new basis for relationships between rich and poor, within and amongst nations.

Despite the shortcomings of the Earth Summit, resulting largely from the political compromises that had to be made to reach consensus, the agreements reached in Rio de Janeiro represent the most comprehensive programme ever agreed by governments for the shaping of the human future. That is still the case. The Declaration of Principles agreed at Rio reaffirmed and built on the Stockholm Conference declaration. The Programme of Action (known as Agenda 21) that the Conference adopted presents a detailed blueprint of the measures required to effect the transition to sustainability. The Conventions on Climate Change and Biodiversity negotiated during the preparations for the Conference were opened for signature and provided the basic legal framework for international agreements on two of the most fundamental global environmental issues. In addition, the Conference agreed an initiating and negotiating process which has since produced a Convention on Desertification, an issue of critical importance to many developing countries, particularly the countries of sub-Saharan Africa, which are amongst the world's poorest. The fact that these were agreed by virtually all of the governments of the world, most of them represented at Rio by their head of government, gives them a unique degree of political authority. But as we have seen, it does not ensure their implementation.

I cannot help but think of a little mistake I made during that Conference. It was a two-week Conference, and in the weekend period between the two weeks I decided to go out to a little restaurant on the outskirts of Rio where nobody would know me. I went out there, and a lady came up to me and said, 'You're Mr Strong'. Well, I admitted it, and did not realize that she was a journalist. She said 'How many world leaders are there actually here?' I said, 'Well, I count about 115 presidents, prime ministers and a few kings,' but then I added indiscreetly, but somewhat accurately, that there were very few leaders. Unhappily my observation was true; and it remains true. Every country in the world has a leader, and yet leadership today is one of the most scarce commodities in the world that cries out for enlightened constructive leadership.

So far the record of Rio is mixed. I need not document here the many evidences of continued environmental deterioration, depletion of forests and of fish stocks, accelerated extinction of species of wildlife and genetic stock, growing pressures on biological resources, and impending shortages of fresh water for human use, which have been well reported in the publications of the United Nations Environment Programme, the World Resources report, and scientific journals. I must make clear that I accept the preponderance of evidence that overall the condition of the earth's environment and the basis for achievement of sustainability continue to deteriorate.

Nevertheless, there have been many positive achievements which demonstrate that the transition called for at Rio is possible. The Conventions on Climate Change, Biodiversity and Desertification have come into international legal force, but progress towards agreement on the protocols necessary to give them teeth has been disappointingly slow. The differences in the perceptions and interests of industrialized and developing countries which made these Conventions so difficult to negotiate continue to inhibit progress on their implementation. The root of most of the differences is the insistence of developing countries that the more industrialized countries, which have been largely responsible for creating these global environmental issues, accept principal responsibility for addressing them, particularly in providing the additional financial resources to cover the costs of implementing the international agreements.

The Global Environment Facility (GEF), established as a result of the Earth Summit, is an innovative mechanism for financing the incremental costs of meeting these needs. It has been notably successful and effective, but its resources are limited. Official development assistance has actually declined, and deeply entrenched differences over intellectual property rights in respect of the biological resources of development countries have brought negotiations on implementation of the Biodiversity Convention, particularly in relation to a Biosafety Protocol to a virtual standstill.

At the meeting of the Conference of the Parties (the signatory states) to the Climate Change Convention in Kyoto, Japan, in 1997, agreement was reached on a broad set of targets and timetables for reduction of greenhouse gas emissions. It now seems evident that most industrialized countries will not meet these targets, and there is little sign at present of the degree of public support and political will that would be required to change this. In the principal countries to which we must look for leadership on these issues—the United States, Canada, members of the European Union and Japan—these concerns have regrettably moved down on the list of priorities. It is not easy to engage the attention of the elite and privileged of these societies on the need for radical changes in the *status quo*, especially with stockmarkets and executive salaries at record levels. For them, there is little incentive to change. None the less, there are some very promising examples of successful change. For example, some 3,000 cities and towns throughout the world have adopted their own Agenda 21 based on the Earth Summit's Global Agenda 21. A number of industry associations and many companies have adopted their versions of Agenda 21; for example the World Tourism and Travel Council, representing the world's largest, and one of its most rapidly growing and environmentally-sensitive industries, and the International Road Transport Union.

There has been widespread adoption of measures which enhance energy efficiency and improve the intensity of energy used both in industrialized and developing countries—perhaps most remarkably in China. In the United States, savings equivalent to some 10 million barrels of oil per day have been realized since 1973 through conservation measures. Technological advances have permitted significant reductions in the energy and material content of many production processes and products. And the most notable example of a successful international agreement in dealing with a major global environmental risk is, of course, the Montreal Protocol. This provided for, and has largely achieved, the phasing out of the use of chlorofluorocarbons, the principle source of atmospheric ozone depletion. It is a sign that progress is feasible when the political will exists. The World Business Council for Sustainable Development documents the impressive achievements of many of its members (comprising some of the world's leading corporations) in improving their environmental performance. It also demonstrates that eco-efficiency (efficiency in the use of materials and energy, and in the prevention, disposal and recycling of waste) is often a source of significant profits rather than of added cost.

In his book, *A Moment on the Earth*, environmental journalist Greg Easterbrook (1995) strikes a responsive chord in many when he makes the case for more environmental optimism. And in a recent article in *World Watch* magazine, Lester Brown expressed his belief that we are approaching a paradigm shift in environmental consciousness that will facilitate the fundamental changes we need to make. There is also some evidence that governments are starting to move again. Several European countries have begun the process of tax shifting: reducing income taxes while off-setting these cuts with higher taxes on environmentally destructive activities.

Finally, there is the robustness of the civil society movement and the greater sophistication of environmental NGOs in making more impact on public attitudes and political will. This has been evidenced by their effective efforts to counter attempts by the OECD to negotiate a multilateral agreement on investment, and of course the protests at the 2000 World Trade Organization in Seattle. We fully expect that we will see more of our NGO friends out in the streets for future protests. I am not sure whether I should be with them or on the outside, but everyone must make a choice sometimes. Working on the same issues with the same values, you can choose sometimes to try and work from the inside as well as from the outside, and I have done a bit of both.

There is therefore some evidence that a paradigm shift may be occurring, but the time available to us to make the radical shift to which Rio pointed is, in my belief, running short. Fundamental change does not come quickly or easily. Despite progress, we continue along a pathway that is not sustainable while the driving forces of population growth in developing countries and unsustainable patterns of production and consumption persist in industrialized countries.

FOOD SECURITY

Even with the profound changes driven by technology, the twenty-first century is likely to see the re-emergence of some very basic traditional issues with significant potential for conflict: access to water, land, resources and livelihoods. The competition for these will intensify. One issue in respect of which we have become dangerously complacent is food security. A recent review of international agricultural research in which I had the opportunity to participate was carried out under the auspices of that unique international network, the Consultative Group for International Agricultural Research. It made the case for a greatly strengthened cooperative programme of scientific and policy research to ensure that the revolutionary advances in biotechnology, that will radically change traditional patterns of food production, and the movement to accord new technologies intellectual property rights, will benefit the poor and do not, as they threaten now to do, impose on the poor a new generation of risks and vulnerabilities.

I am convinced that governance—the ability to manage this complex of forces through which we are shaping our future—is going to be the primary challenge we face in the twenty-first century. The system of cause and effect, through which human policies and activities have their impacts on the processes that are shaping our future, is indeed systemic. As significant dimensions of space and time often separate cause and effect, the real consequences are not always readily discernible. The overall magnitude of human activities which impact on the natural ecological and life support systems of the earth is often relatively small in relation to natural forces, as, for example, in the build-up of greenhouse gases in the atmosphere. But they can nevertheless have a profound, and indeed perhaps decisive, impact on the complex set of natural balances on which human life and well-being depend, which have developed over aeons of time, and which could move us beyond the margins of safety and sustainability. Management of our impacts on this system is the main challenge of governance as I see it, and it is in this sense that I use the term.

GOVERNANCE AND THE FUTURE

To manage these impacts effectively cannot simply be a matter of placing our bets on the predictions of experts, however plausible they may be. I am told that a survey done by the American Association for the Advancement of Science in the 1930s of new technologies that may impact on society did not actually identify a single one of the technologies that now dominate our life. We have to have a view of the future, but we have to be careful not to fix that view on a set of predictions. We have in effect to prepare for a future that we cannot reliably predict. Of course we must understand the processes by which human activities interact with each other and with natural phenomena to produce their ultimate consequences. We must know at what points and in what ways our interventions in these systems can have the effects we desire. This means, too, that we must know what we desire, what risks we want to avoid, what opportunities we seek to expand, and what limits or boundary conditions we must accept to ensure a sustainable and secure future.

We are the first generation in history of which it is true that we are literally the agents of our own future. What we do, or fail to do, is actually determining our future, so we must understand these processes. We must understand how our interventions in them can affect them positively, and of course negatively. This does not require homogeneity in our lifestyles or aspirations. It does require at the global level that we agree on those measures which are essential in avoiding the major risks to survival and well-being of the human community, while ensuring the broadest range of opportunities for individual self-expression and fulfilment. It is instructive to remind ourselves that the most healthy and sustainable natural ecological systems are those which maintain the highest degree of diversity and variety. But to ensure their sustainability requires that they remain within certain basic boundary conditions on which the health and effective functioning of the systems depend. The same, I would contend, is true of human systems. The essence of human freedom surely lies in the extent to which individuals have the largest range of choices as to how they want to live their lives and are prepared to accept the disciplines that make it possible for them to enjoy the benefits of technology.

There has been no more liberating technology than the automobile, yet look at the constraints that we face in using it. In order to use it effectively we have to accept a number of disciplines and restraints. We have to be able to confine ourselves to one side of the road, to stop at red lights, to do a whole series of other things. To enjoy the benefits of air travel we have to suffer the indignities of going through personal searches. We have accepted all these because we realize that we have to make a trade-off between the enlarged opportunities that new technologies provide to us and the disciplines that we have to accept to be able to enjoy them.

The processes through which human activities produce their ultimate consequences transcend the traditional boundaries of nations, sectors, and disciplines. People are realizing now how their lives are being affected by decisions being made by expert organizations like the World Trade Organization and the International Monetary Fund. These are very professional, very skilled, competent organizations. But their decisions are being made within narrow institutional mandates, without the participation of those who are highly impacted by their decisions. That kind of governance will not work. If people's lives are being affected by expert decisions in which they have not had an opportunity to participate, they are not going to accept them. That is why the UN and the international system of organizations must function more as a system. We call the UN a system, but it is not very systemic. The UN is not a world government. It is a servant of nation states. It does only those things that its member nation states warrant, and give it the right and the resources to undertake specific sets of activity. National governments themselves are often fragmented. But most have ministries within the framework of a cabinet system, where they can reconcile various differences, at least in principle. That's not so true in the UN. Every specialized agency of the UN is autonomous. It is separately financed by governments, it has its own governing body, and it does not have to respond to the leadership of the Secretary General, who is effect the prime minister of the international multilateral system.

So although the complex processes through which human actions are shaping the human future are systemic in nature, the institutions through which we attempt to manage these are far from systemic. Governments and industry are organized primarily on a sectoral basis, and academia on the basis of individual disciplines. Sectoral organization is not easy to achieve in universities. Very often university people in their own specialized areas can better get together in institutions outside the university.

Despite a great deal of talk about the need for more systemic, integrated and multi-disciplinary approaches to management and decision-making, and some useful but limited progress in this direction, there is still a vast dis-connect between our current management and decision making processes and the real world cause-and-effect system on which it impacts. This dichotomy must be addressed if we are to develop a sustainable system of governance. The multilateral organizations, including the UN, are not sufficiently prepared for the new generation of tasks that are required of them. They have many deficiencies, but frankly they would be impossible to invent today, given the current political climate: if an agreement on the UN Charter were attempted today, there would never be success. That is why reform is so difficult.

I helped Secretary General Kofi Annan with his restructuring of the UN. He presented two sets of proposals, one in the areas in which he, as the Chief Executive Officer, had the authority to move. We called that Track One. The second were those things where he could only recommend that governments take action. The Track One proposals have all been implemented in one fashion or another. Some might argue perhaps not as well as they might be, but nevertheless he has carried out more reform than has ever before been experienced in the UN. Yet not one of the fundamental proposals for change that he recommended that governments take has in fact been undertaken. So you can see that the very governments which in their rhetoric call for reform of the UN offer the greatest resistance to real reform. One of the reasons is that the shape of the international multilateral system today very much reflects the geopolitics of the world that emerged from World War II. Yet the geopolitical landscape has changed fundamentally, with developing countries representing some 75 per cent of the world's nations, and roughly about the same percentage of its people. They are also well on the way to representing more than 50 per cent of the GNP of the world. Despite this importance, only one developing country, China, is amongst the five members of the Security Council.

Although I am a great friend of the United Kingdom, and my roots long ago were here, realistically Britain is no longer in that league of political significance. Neither Britain nor France will be amongst the top industrialized countries measured by GNP within the next 15 years or so, and my country, Canada, will not be there either. *The Economist* projects that in the year 2020 9 of the 15 major countries will in fact be developing countries in economic terms. We have to get used to the fact we are a minority.

We have to be willing to allow the institutions of the world, and particularly the UN and the World Bank, to reflect that fact. Are we really ready to let democracy function on a global level?

The country that is the greatest promulgator of democracy in the world is the United States, the neighbour country where I actually spend more of my time than I do in Canada. I have great regard for the United States, but I keep challenging US audiences: 'Are you, as the great champion of democracy, prepared to let democracy function on a global basis?' I usually get silence in response to that, because the fact is that not only the United States, but also those who have dominated the multilateral institutions since the end of World War II, including the UK and France, are simply reluctant to give up their privileged status. However, today's *unrealism* becomes tomorrow's inevitability. Inertia will often carry institutional arrangements well beyond the time when they have outdated their original reasons. We will have to accommodate to a world in which we are a privileged minority—a powerful minority, yes, but nevertheless a minority. We are a long way from recognizing that.

The future of the world environment will be largely determined by what happens in the developing world, particularly Asia. They will be influenced by our example more than by our rhetoric, and we are not, at this point, setting a very good example. They will also be influenced by the investments we are prepared to make in helping them to contribute to a more sustainable world. It is less expensive to reduce carbon dioxide emissions in developing countries than it is in many of our countries. It is dangerous to carry that too far, but nevertheless the willingness to offset emissions of carbon dioxide that we produce by paying developing countries to undertake projects in their countries, including projects involving preservation of 'sinks' of tropical forests, can result in a much more cost-effective way of reducing overall global emissions. At the same time it can provide a new source of income for developing countries—but one in which they cannot go too far in utilizing. It would be wrong for us to induce them to sell a precious asset, the absorptive capacity of their environment, too cheaply or too soon. So there is risk in this as there is in everything else.

MAINTAINING PEACE AND SECURITY

Maintaining world peace and security was the principal motivation for the creation of the UN in the aftermath of the devastation of World War II. It continues to be at the centre of the UN's global mission as the prerequisite for the achievement of all other goals to which the human community aspires in the twenty-first century. Although the risks of global nuclear war have receded since the demise of the Cold War, a proliferation of ethnic and regional conflicts is exacting a heavy cost in terms of human lives, suffering and economic deprivation in many parts of the world. The need to develop a culture of peace is articulated in a resolution of a recent UN General Assembly, and the underlying conditions for prevention of conflicts and their peaceful resolution is a fundamental precondition for the achievement of a sustainable civilization. Peace and sustainability are two sides of the same coin.

I will not mention population except to acknowledge the fact that despite lowered rates of population growth, we are in fact faced with a growing world population concentrated largely in developing countries. It may level off sometime in this century that we have just begun, perhaps somewhere in the mid-part of the century, but at a level that is probably going to be some 50 per cent or so higher than it is now. In any event, it is going to add significantly to the pressures. There are changing demographics of a different nature in the more mature industrialized countries. In Japan, if the present rates continue the population will be zero in something like 80 years. We are facing a very major demographic divide. As our industrialized countries become more mature, and the population ages and declines, the pressures for inward flows are going to be tremendous, because people all over the world will be knocking at our doors.

It used to be that emigration provided a real solution to the pressures of excess populations, at a time when those population levels were much less than they are today. But today the borders of the world are closing, except to the rich and privileged who are invited everywhere with their money. To the poor and the underprivileged the borders of the world are closing, and the pressures that are building up behind those borders are going to impinge on all of us. Canada is a little colder, a little harder to get to than some, but even so, today, boatloads of people from places like China are slipping into our country. Europe has a turbulent east, the Middle East, and also North Africa, all looking to Europe. There will be more and more pressure. I keep saying to my Canadian friends: 'Is history going to be sufficient to validate our claim as Canadians to have a disproportionate share of the world's territory and its resources?' In the twenty-first century will those norms be recognized by a world in which the needs for territory, the needs for livelihoods, the needs for land and resources are going to be escalating? Now can we really maintain the *status quo*? The rules will change—necessity changes rules and mores. The mores of international life that accept the principle of national sovereignty will be affected by this immense build-up of pressures .

Developing countries are contributing more and more to the larger global risks of climate change, ozone depletion, degradation of biological resources, and loss or deterioration of arable lands. China has already become the second largest single source of carbon dioxide emissions, and will almost certainly succeed the United States to the dubious honour of becoming number one. The prospect is for a massive increase in third-world energy consumption over the next thirty years. Much of the expansion will be in countries like India and China, where by their own projections coal use will increase by more than 60 per cent in India and 50 per cent in China. Industrialized countries have largely created these problems, although developing countries will become the primary contributors to the growing pressures. Yet can we really properly deny them the right to grow? It would be wrong for us to constrain the growth of developing countries: they too have a right to grow. We must join with them in helping to ensure that their growth is sustainable. That requires assistance which we should not look at as charity, but rather as an investment in global environmental security and sustainability. It is an investment that we will simply have to make.

Recently, I was in China, and I met amongst others Prime Minister Ju Rong Ji. He spent the whole hour talking about the lessons that he had learnt through the mistakes that China has made in mismanagement of its environment. He focused particularly on the devastating effects of the Yangtse floods, which were attributable to the fact that trees along the watersheds feeding into the Yangtse had been cut down. He said, 'I'm going to make sure that we double our tree planting in the next ten years. Personally, I am going to spend the rest of my life planting trees, even after I leave the prime ministership.' Well, that is something coming from the premier of China! He seemed to mean it, and the very fact that he said it was itself significant. As you know, the air pollution levels in places like Beijing and New Delhi are inflicting tremendous impacts on human health. The developing countries I find are becoming very environmentally sensitive, not because they have heard us talking about it, but because they are experiencing the problems themselves.

A NEW ECOS-NOMICS

Developing countries are the custodians of some of the most important life-support mechanisms of our planet, biological diversity being a major example. These perform services which, if they were taken into account in our economies, would be worth vast amounts of money to us. We must start valuing those services. Likewise, we must start incorporating the prices of products we get from developing countries into our financial and economic relations with them—to give full recognition of the environmental and social costs that they include. That is not easy and cannot be done just through the trading system: it requires a system that recognizes those costs.

To put it a bit simplistically: the earth needs to be run like a corporation, with a depreciation and a maintenance account. In other words, the earth's assets must be maintained. Much of what we have counted as GNP increase over the years has actually been running down capital. Yet if we accounted on that basis we would have to accord value to these essential services, and that would help to bring the developing countries into a more real partnership of the kind that is necessary.

The fact that most flows of funds these days to developing countries come in the form of private investment rather than official development assistance means that we cannot help them in their transition to sustainability unless we affect how corporations and investors invest. That again requires some specific action in establishing incentives. People respond to incentives. Corporations respond to incentives. The Earth Council did a study which made it very clear that in four sectors there were over $700 billion of annual subsidies which primarily subsidized unsustainable practices that not only imposed immense costs on the environment, but at the same time immense economic costs on people as tax payers and consumers. If you change the system of incentives and penalties that motivate economic behaviour you will get a response. We have to start giving positive incentives to sustainability, and we have seen that it is possible, but it will only happen if governments provide the motivation.

I would like to make a couple of suggestions of how I feel a new system of governance might function. One of the key elements, in my view, must be a viable system of governance at the global level. *It does not need to be a world government and should not be.* The world is not ready for it. It needs, however, to be a system of governance through which collectively we can manage the impacts that determine our future cooperatively in those areas where we simply cannot do it alone.

The UN is the indispensable centrepiece of this system. It needs significant change, which, however difficult, can come much more readily than the attempt to recreate it. It also has to bring in the other actors. We did something in preparation for the Earth Summit that worked very well. We recognized that the UN is a forum. It is a place where issues can be negotiated: it is not the place where operations can be undertaken to deal with them. So we brought in the other actors. We brought in corporations and other agencies outside the UN, like the OECD. We brought in professional associations. The UN needs to do that more and more. It needs to recognize that the levers that determine the major issues that are shaping our future are in a variety of different hands, many of them non-governmental. We need to bring governments and the other actors into networks of issue-related policy systems and decision-making systems. The ingredients for that are beginning to take shape. Kofi Annan in his reform programme called for the establishment of a series of issue management systems, in which the various actors (UN and non-UN, with the UN being the convening actor) could come together in making decisions that affect issues of special global importance.

Here, modern technology, particularly information process technology, provides the tools to understand and manage these systems. But as I mentioned earlier, we are still at a primitive stage in establishing the institutional structures through which we seek to manage them. What will we have to do? Well, first of all we need a new economic paradigm which integrates the disciplines of traditional economics with the new insights of ecological economics, what I call a new *ecos-nomics*. This must provide the theoretical underpinnings for a system that incorporates into economic pricing and national accounts the real values of the environment and services which nature provides. It should also include fiscal and regulatory regimes with positive incentives for the achievement of economic, social and environmental sustainability.

In a market economy which drives the processes of globalization, the market response provides the signals that motivate sustainable development. This means shifting taxes from products and practices which are environmentally and socially beneficial to those which are least harmful. It means, in effect, getting the prices right. And no nation can do this alone without disadvantaging its own industry and consumers. It has to be done through international agreement. There is a lot of room for individuality in the manner in which we administer these nationally, but it must be within an internationally agreed framework. A realignment of the mandates and functions of inter-governmental organizations is needed based on the principles of subsidiarity with well-defined linkages amongst them. In this way they can consult and cooperate more systematically in dealing with issues involving the mandates and capacities of more than one, and that involves bringing the WTO, the IMF, and the World Bank, into a much more closely cooperative system than now. I believe, for example, that the United Nations Secretary General should have a place at the table when major economic crises, like the crisis in Indonesia, are being determined. Someone has to bring the authoritative voice of the social and environmental impacts of those changes to the decisions that are made. They are usually made under the pressures of emergency but have profound and long-term impacts on societies and on the global economy.

Explicit provision needs to be made for ensuring that the environmental and social impacts of economic and financial policies and decisions are taken into full account. A series of regional economic trade and security arrangements within a global framework would complement and support rather than compete with global arrangements. The establishment of a World Environment Organization based on an upgrading of the status of the UN Environment Programme to that of a specialized agency, and according it a strengthened and broader mandate as the focal point for international environmental cooperation, would make it an effective counterpart to the World Trade Organization and the International Monetary Fund in their fields. The Trusteeship Council of the UN is an organ which exists but has outlived its original functions. It should be transformed into the deliberative organ at the highest political levels of the UN, where the nations of the world come together to exercise their collective trusteeship for the global commons.

Global commons issues are going to become major drivers of the environment. The Antarctic, outer space, the atmosphere, the oceans, even the overall life-support system for the Earth itself are, in a sense, common areas. The various elements that come into management of these common areas need to converge into one high-level organization which can take the important political decisions required to safeguard them. An effective international regime for surveillance and regulation of capital movements and the financial institutions through which they flow should be established. This could lead to the IMF evolving into a global central bank. Even great global speculators like George Soros have admitted to the need for the control of international capital flows. Often weaker countries, and even some stronger ones, are at the mercy of international capital flows which they have no basis for controlling or even for anticipating.

We need more effective and systematic mechanisms for the engagement of civil society in inter-governmental forum. Incidentally, some of you may recall an article in *Foreign Affairs* by Lesley Salmon, the social philosopher, which compares the rise of non-governmental organizations in our times to the development of the nation-state system. That may be a little extravagant. They cannot replace the nation-state system, and some of them are of dubious legitimacy and accountability. Nevertheless, as a whole they are a means by which people more and more bring their special insights and interests to the international agenda.

More effective and systematic use of the immense capabilities that technologies provide for transparency surveillance, analysis and early warning would help identify emerging issues, illuminate solutions and monitor performance. It would support an enforceable regime of international law. Here again, I am absolutely persuaded that for an effective, functional global society we must extend into international life the basic system of enforceable law and order which provides the basis for the effective functioning of national societies. We are at the beginning of that. There are a whole series of international agreements, but very little mechanism for enforcement. We need more reliable, consistent financing of international organizations, including the UN. The US, as the only superpower in the world today, can get along better, it sometimes thinks, without the UN, but the rest of the world cannot. I was asked in Canada, as a former Deputy Minister of Foreign Affairs, what can Canada do in the next century? I said, we would have a minor role, but nevertheless an influential role. The United States needs a loyal opposition, not an enemy, and the nations of the world need to come together in the UN and the multilateral system to provide that counterbalance to the unilateral exercise of US power which it has more and more tendency to resort to.

FINAL COMMENT

Commitment to eradication of poverty must be a primary goal of governance in the international system. You cannot have sustainability in environmental terms without sustainability in social terms, which means more equity. For the first time in history, we have the capacity and the means to do it, but lack the will. So many of the ingredients already exist, but have not been put together. This, in my view, is the principal challenge we face in this new century—to be able to develop a viable system of managing this complex of forces by which we are shaping our future, while opening up vast new opportunities for individual self-expression which this accords. The sum total of the behaviour of individuals is the main source of human impacts on the global environment on which all of these risks depend.

Finally, let me simply say that the dominant ethos today is of individual and national self-interest. I hope everyone shares my deep belief that individual rights and freedoms constitute the fundamental foundations of our society. But in order to be able to exercise these rights and freedoms they must be accompanied by acceptance of the disciplines necessary to ensure that all of us can enjoy them, and a high sense of responsibility to each other and to future generations. It is in this sense of shared responsibility that I believe we must reinforce our efforts to ensure a sustainable and secure future. For in the final analysis the behaviour of individuals, as well as the priorities of society, responds not only to our narrow economic and security interests, important as these are, but also ultimately to the deepest moral, ethical and spiritual values of people. All of our diligent work in devising new policies, new programmes, and new international agreements in this new millennium will remain. But they will be unfulfilled designs and aspirations unless we have the collective motivation to give them priority in our own lives and in our own political agendas. At this stage of my life, having spent so many years dealing with these issues, I believe that it is the will—the motivation to act—that is the key missing element. Only if that motivation changes will we actually be able to use the awesome tools that science and technology now provide us, to permit us to understand and manage our affairs on this planet. We must raise our motivations beyond the individual and national interests that divide us to our broader common interest in a sustainable future. This must guide us in the management of those activities that shape our future.

One of my greatest disappointments in the results of the Earth Summit was our inability to obtain agreement on an Earth Charter. The Charter would have defined a set of basic moral and ethical principles for the conduct of people and nations towards each other and the earth for as basis for achieving a sustainable way of life on our planet. I proposed this, and urged it to the world leaders gathered in Rio. They were not ready for it.

The Earth Council has joined with many other organizations around the world to undertake this important piece of unfinished business from Rio. This is being done through a global campaign designed to stimulate dialogue and enlist contributions of people everywhere to the formulation of a People's Earth Charter—in the Anglo-Saxon tradition, a sort of Magna Carta for the earth. The process itself is releasing tremendous energies, and the authority of this will not be that of a signed treaty by governments, but that which comes from the process with millions of people already participating in it. It is intended to be a compelling and authoritative voice of the world's people, which hopefully will have a powerful and persuasive influence on governments.

I am persuaded, then, that the twenty-first century will be decisive for our species. The direction of the human future will be largely set in the first few decades that we have now started. All the evidences of environmental degradation, social tension, and inter-communal conflict to date have occurred at levels of population and human activities that are a great deal less than they will be in this new century. The risks we face in common from the mounting dangers to the environmental resource base and life-support systems of our earth are far greater now, as we move into this new century than the risks we face, or have ever faced, in our conflicts with each other. A new paradigm of cooperative global governance is the only feasible basis on which we can manage these risks and realize the immense potential for progress and fulfilment for the entire human family: this is now within our reach. All people and nations have, in the past, been willing to accord the highest priority to measures required for their own security. If action is carried out in the name of security, the political will and the resources will follow. We must understand that we face a different and more complex security issue today. We must give the same kind of priority to civilization security and sustainability that we have always given to military security. This will take a major shift in the current political mindset, but history perhaps sounds a note of optimism by telling us that necessity will compel such a shift eventually. So the real question is, can we really afford the costs and the risks of waiting?

REFERENCES

Brundtland, G. H. (1987). *Our Common Future*. World Commission on Environment and Development, chaired by Gro Harlem Bruntland. Oxford: Oxford University Press.

Carson, R. (1963). *Silent Spring*. London: Hamish Hamilton.

Easterbrook, G. (1995). *A Moment on the Earth : The Coming Age of Environmental Optimism*. London: Penguin.

Marsh, G. P. (1864). *Man And Nature; Or, Physical Geography As Modified by Human Action*. New York.

Meadows, H. *et al*. (1972). *The Limits to Growth : A Report for the Club of Rome's Project on the Predicament of Mankind*. London: Earth Island.

Department of the Environment, UK (1988). *Our Common Future: A Perspective by the United Kingdom on the Report of the World Commission on Environment and Development*. London.

8

Fragmenting Cosmic Connections: Converting Nature Into Commodity

Darrell Addison Posey

MOST contributions to this volume frame emerging 'consciousness of connections' through international politics, economics and trade, urban/ rural exchanges, social movements, environmental transformations, and global citizenship and governance. These views reflect a remarkably *linear* world-view of dialectics such as: past/present, growth/sustainability, internal/external, and production/recycle. Langton (Chapter 9), however, introduces the idea of symbolic environmental space, or *spacialization*, which is expressed in the Aboriginal concept of *totem*. *Totem* defines other dimensions of knowing that emerge from cosmic environments through connections with animal spirits. These non-lineal manifestations might be described as spiritual *clusters* that, unlike the electron clouds that enshroud an atomic nucleus, are literally grounded through centres that define human landscapes marked by cultural mechanisms such as sacred sites and song lines.

Indigenous peoples in other parts of the world share with Aboriginal Australians this view of cosmic connectedness between living things and the Earth (see Posey and Dutfield 1996). Thus, human beings share life with all other living organisms, and, indeed, may be transformed into other transgenic forms through death, ceremony, or shamanistic practice. In this chapter, I want to explore how such world-views function to create and maintain anthropogenic and cultural landscapes that conserve ecological and biological diversity. I also hope to show how global trade and political initiatives are working to sever and fragment these cosmic connections by reducing the vast bio-diversity of nature to mere products for biotechnology and commercial exploitation.

I suggest that the commodification of nature—especially through Intellectual Property Rights (IPRs)—is one of the biggest threats to global security in the twenty-first century. This is because global consumerism is driven by market prices that ignore or obliterate the local cultural, spiritual and economic values of indigenous and local peoples, who still manage, maintain and conserve much of the biological diversity of the planet.

Many of my examples will come from the Kayapó Indians, with whom I have lived and worked since 1977. The Kayapó inhabit a 4 million hectare (approximately 9 million acre) continuum of ecosystems from the grass-lands of the Brazilian *planalto* to the tropical and gallery forests of the Amazon basin. They speak a language of the Jê linguistic family and are noted for their complex social structure and political organization (see Posey 1982, 1990, 1997).

BACKGROUND

Many of the areas of highest biological diversity on the planet are inhabited by indigenous and traditional peoples, providing what the Declaration of Belém calls an 'inextricable link' between biological and cultural diversity (Posey and Overal 1990). In fact, of the nine countries which together account for 60 per cent of human languages, six of these 'centres of cultural diversity' are also 'mega(bio)diversity' countries with exceptional num-bers of unique plant and animal species (Durning 1992: 6)

It is estimated that there are currently at least 300 million people world-wide who are indigenous. These diverse groups occupy a wide geograph-ical range from the polar regions to the deserts, savannas and forests of tropical zones. According to UNESCO (1993), 4,000 to 5,000 of the 6,000 languages remaining in the world are spoken by indigenous peoples, implying that indigenous groups still constitute most of the world's cul-tural and linguistic diversity.

Indigenous peoples have increasingly become the focus for research aimed at the development of new products or the improvement of medi-cines, agricultural products, body and skin preparations, natural oils, essences, dyes, and insecticides. They have long been targets for expropri-ation of their music, art, crafts, and images. Trade has removed materials, ideas, expressions of culture—and even human genes—from their social and spiritual contexts to convert them into *objects* for commercial exploitation. This process often results in disrespect for other cultures or violation of basic human rights.

Although conservation and management practices are highly pragmatic, indigenous peoples generally view knowledge as emanating from a spirit-ual base. All creation is sacred, and the sacred and secular are inseparable. Spirituality is the highest form of consciousness, and spiritual consciousness is the highest form of awareness. In this sense, a dimension of traditional knowledge is not *local* knowledge, but knowledge of the *universal* as expressed in (or revealed through) the local.

Experts exist who are peculiarly aware of nature's organizing principles, that are sometimes described as entities or spirits, or by cosmic law (these specialists are usually referred to as shamans by anthropologists). Knowledge of the environment depends not only on the relationship between humans and nature, but also between the visible world and the invisible spirit world. Thus, the unseen is as much a part of society as that which is seen—the spiritual is as much a part of reality as the material. In fact, there is a complementary relationship between the two, *with the spiritual being more powerful than the material.* Behind visible objects lie essences that constitute the true nature of those objects.

Indigenous peoples frequently view themselves as guardians and stewards of nature. Harmony and equilibrium are central concepts in most cosmologies. Agriculture, for example, can provide 'balance for well-being' through relationships not only among people, but also nature and deities. In this concept, the blessing of a new field represents not mere spectacle, but an inseparable part of life where the highest value is harmony with the Earth. Most traditions recognize linkages between health, diet, properties of different foods and medicinal plants, and horticultural/natural resource management practices—all within a highly articulated cosmological/social context. The plant, animal, or crystal some ethnopharmacologist or scientist wants to collect, may, in fact, encompass, contain, or actually be the manifestation of ancestral spirits—or even of the local healers' own progenitors.

Local knowledge embraces information about location, movements, and other factors explaining spatial patterns and timing in the ecosystem, including sequences of events, cycles, and trends. Direct links with the land are fundamental and obligations to maintain those connections form the core of individual and group identity. Nowhere is that more apparent than with the dreaming-places of the Aboriginal peoples of Australia. As James Yunupingu, chairperson of the Northern Land Council, explains: 'My land is mine only because I came in spirit from that land, and so did my ancestors of the same land. My land is my foundation.'

The Cherokee of North America see themselves as being an integral part of the Earth. Thus a dam does not just flood the land, but destroys the medicines and the knowledge of the medicines associated with the land. As one healer explained: 'If we are to make our offerings at a new place, the spiritual beings would not know us. We would not know the mountains or the significance of them. We would not know the land and the land would not know us. . . . We would not know the sacred places. . . . If we were to go on top of an unfamiliar mountain we would not know the life forms that dwell there.'

The same is true for the Mazatecs of Southern Mexico, whose shamans and *curandeiros* confer with the plant spirits in order to heal. Successful curers must above all else learn to listen to their plants (Harrison 1999). For many groups, these communications come through the transformative powers of altered states or trances. Don Hilde, a Pucallpa healer, explains: 'I did not have a teacher to help me learn about [healing] plants, but visions have taught me many things. They even instruct me as to which . . . medicines to use' (Dobkin de Rios 1992: 146).

These links between life, land, and society are identified as the 'sacred balance'. As Science with its quantum mechanics methods inadequately addresses the universe as a whole; and it certainly can never adequately describe the holism of indigenous knowledge and belief. In fact, science is far behind in the environmental movement. It still sees nature as objects for human use and exploitation ('components' of biodiversity is the term used in the Convention on Biological Diversity; see Strong, this volume).

Furthermore, technology uses the banner of scientific 'objectivity' to mask the moral and ethical issues that emerge from such a functionalist, anthropocentric philosophy. Marilyn Strathern (1996) makes this clear when discussing the ethical dilemmas raised (or avoided) when embryos are 'decontextualized' as human beings to become 'objects' of scientific research. For indigenous peoples, removal of life forms and knowledge from their cosmic connections evokes exactly the same moral indignation as experimentation with foetuses does in our society. This is because the many 'components' of nature for indigenous peoples are extensions of human society (e.g., *totems* for the Aboriginal Peoples of Australia). This is fundamentally difficult for Western society to understand, since, for us, the extension of 'self' is through 'hard technology', not through nature (Martins 1993).

This is elucidated in the Kayapó myth, 'The Journey to Become a Shaman' (see Posey 1982):

Listen! Those who become sick from strong fevers lie in death's position; they lie as though they are dead. The truly great ones, the truly strong person who is a *wayanga*, shows the sick how to leave their bodies. They leave through their insides. They pass through their insides and come to be in the form of a stone. Their bodies lie as in death, but beyond they are then transformed into an armadillo. As an armadillo, they assume good, strong health and they pass through the other side, over there (pointing to the east).

Then they become a bat and fly—*ko,ko,ko,ko,ko* (the noise of flying). Then they go further beyond in the form of a dove. They fly like a dove—*ku,ku,ku,ku* (the sound of a dove's flight). They join the other *wayangas* and all go together.

'Where will we go? What is the way? Go to the east, way over there.' *Ku, ku, ku, ku* . . .

And way over there is a spider's web. Some go round and round near the spider's web and they just sit (permanently). The true and ancient shamans must teach them how to fly through the web. But those who have not been shown how try to break through the web and the web grabs their wings thus (the narrator wraps his arms around his shoulders). They just hang in the web and die. Their bodies are carried by their relatives and are buried without waiting, for the spider's web has entangled them, wrapped up their wings , and they are dead.

Those who have been caused to know themselves, however, go round the spider web. They sit on the mountain seat of the shamans and sing like the dove— *tu,tu,tu,tu*. They acquire the knowledge of the ancestors. They speak to the spirits of all the animals and of the ancestors. They know (all).

They then return (to their bodies). They return to their homes. They enter and they breathe.

And the others say: He arrived! He arrived! He arrived! He arrived!

And the women all wail: '*Ayayikakraykyerekune*' (He has arrived).

And the shaman says: 'Do not bury me, I am still alive. I am a *wayanga*. I am now one who can cure: I am the one who smokes the powerful pipe. I know how to go through my body and under my head. I am a *wayanga*.'

The story is centred around the capability of the *wayanga* to leave his/her body (*kà*) and be transformed into other cosmic forms. Energy (*karon*) can be stored temporarily in rocks, but inevitably gets transformed into armadillos, doves or bats. (Note that the human spirit can inhabit these sequentially through a type of 'transgenic migration'.)

The spider's web represents the barrier between the visible and invisible worlds. Armadillos are persistent animals that know to burrow under the web; doves are powerful flyers and can break right through the barrier; while bats are such skilful fliers that they manoeuvre through the strands.

The sounds of the dove's and bat's flights represent the different frequencies that their vibrations impart. Frequencies have associated sounds and colours. Just to analyse the variations in frequencies of bee sounds would require discussing the fifty-two different folk species of stingless bee, each of which has a distinctive sound and curative properties.

The most powerful shamans can transform themselves into not just one of the animals, but all of them. And, once on the other side of the spider's web, after they have passed through the endless dark chasm, they enter into the spectral frequencies of different light (or colours). There is a different spectral frequency for each animal (*mry-karon*). The general term for undifferentiated energy is *karon*. Defined energies are given distinctive modifiers (x-*karon*) , where x-might be *mry* for animals (*mry-karon*), *tep* for fish, or *kwen* for birds, etc.

Some shamans only learn the secrets of a few animals and their energies, while others 'know all' (in the words of the myth). They have learned about all of the spectral frequencies and their respective animal energies. Upon return to their bodies, the *wayanga* begin to 'work' (*nhipex*) with the animal energies encountered in their transformation.

The basis of the 'work' is to maintain a balance between animal energies and human energies. Eating the meat of, coming in contact with, or even dreaming about animals can cause an imbalance in these energies, as can, of course, a well-elaborated list of anti-social actions. *Wayanga* use a great variety of techniques for restoring balance (they can also create imbalances—kanê—that lead to sickness), but plants are the most common 'mediators' that manipulate this balance (Posey and Elisabetksy 1991).

Plants themselves have energies (*karon*), but do not have distinctive energies or spirits (*x-karon*), except for some of the *mekrakindja* ('child-want-thing', plants that aid in conception). These plants have very powerful spirits and cause the user to dream of a child's conception. Men and women use these dreaming plants, although men are usually the ones who first 'see' (*kra pumunh*) the child in a dream (Elisabetsky and Posey 1989).

Other plants also have spirits (i.e., defined energies or *x-karon*), especially the *metykdja* ('the poison plants'), the *meudjy* ('witchcraft plants'), and the most deadly and powerful *pitu* (no direct translation). These plants cause drastic alterations to human beings, such as death, paralysis, blindness, insanity, abortion, etc. Even less powerful plants have qualities that can either harm or help the balance between human and animal energies (*me-karon* and *mry-karon*)—indeed, it appears that all plants have curative values. The Kayapó have no question about their existence and future health being dependent upon plants and animals and the forces of nature.

Normally spirits of the dead pass easily into the other world (*mekaron nhon pyka*) and continue their existence in what is roughly the mirror image of what goes on in this world. 'Deceased' (they never really die, for they have already died and just disappear and reappear) *wayanga* live in a special cave in the mountains—thus the reference in the myth about becoming a shaman to their mountain seat. Spirits of dead animals also go to the 'the other world'. Devoted pets are sometimes killed and buried with their 'owners' at death, so that the human spirit will not be so lonely. (Some Kayapó say that dogs are buried with their owners because the dogs can help the human spirit find its way to the 'other world'.)

Those who attempt a shamanistic transformation and do not succeed, however, have a more tragic end. Their spirits are lost forever in the spider's web. There is disagreement among the Kayapó as to what this really means, but there is no doubt that it is the worst possible fate. There is little wonder that only a small portion of the Kayapó population have ever tried to become a *wayanga*.

Kwyra-kà , a shaman/mentor, showed great concern when the first coffin arrived in Gorotire and his nephew was buried in it instead of the traditional manner. (The Kayapó traditionally bury the body in a crouched position in deep, round pits, covered with logs and soil. Until recently, secondary burial was practised four days after principal burial. This allowed time for the spirit to return to the body in case the 'dead' person was only on a shamanistic journey.) He anguished over the possibility that the soul of the child would not be able to escape from the casket to the other world.

Likewise, Kayapós have expressed their deep concerns with the plants that were taken during ethnobotanical surveys to be pressed and dried in herbaria. They are concerned with what happens to the plants' energies. If the plants were kept in such closed, sterile places, would their spirits be trapped, thereby provoking an imbalance and danger to the Kayapó, as well as those who 'kept' them? Like the casket containing the small child, would the energy not become imprisoned, thereby blocking the 'natural' cycles? Even deeper concerns are expressed about the massive quantities of plants that would have to be collected to provide the oils, essences, colourings, and the like for commercialization of plant products. The *wayanga* ask: 'Has anyone ever consulted the plants?' Would the dreaming that is necessary for conception of healthy children be jeopardized? Would the plants stop mediating between the human and animal '*karons*', thereby leading to loss of ancient cures and provoking new diseases? These are the concerns that underlie Kayapó natural resource management practices and provide the 'inextricable link' that connects indigenous peoples with the cosmos.

CULTURAL LANDSCAPES AND BIODIVERSITY CONSERVATION

Western science may have invented the words 'nature', 'biodiversity', and 'sustainability', but it certainly did not initiate the concepts. Indigenous, traditional and local communities have sustainably utilized and conserved a vast diversity of plants, animals, and ecosystems for millennia. Furthermore, human beings have moulded environments through their conscious and unconscious activities—to the extent that it is often impossible to separate nature from culture.

Some recently 'discovered' cultural landscapes include those of Aboriginal peoples, who, 100,000 years before the term 'sustainable development' was coined, were trading seeds, dividing tubers, and propagating domesticated and non-domesticated plant species. Sacred sites act as conservation areas for vital water sources and individual species by restricting access and behaviour. Traditional technologies, including fire use, were part of extremely sophisticated systems that shaped and maintained the balance of vegetation and wildlife. Decline of fire management and loss of sacred sites, when Aboriginal people were centralized into settlements, led to rapid decline of mammals throughout the arid regions (Sultan, Craig and Ross 1997).

Another example of 'cultural landscapes' are the 'forest islands' (*apêtê*) of the Kayapó Indians of Brazil (Posey 1985; 1990; 1997). Kayapó practices of planting and transplanting within and between many ecological zones indicate the degree to which indigenous presence has modified Amazonia. Extensive plantations of fruit and nut trees, as well as 'forest islands' (*apêtê*) created in savanna, force scientists to re-evaluate what have often hastily and erroneously been considered 'natural' Amazonian landscapes. The Kayapó techniques of constructing *apêtê* in savanna show the degree to which this Amazon group can create and manipulate micro-environments within and between ecozones to actually increase biological diversity. Such ecological engineering requires a detailed knowledge of soil fertility, micro-climatic properties and plant varietal qualities, as well as inter-relationships between components of a human-modified ecological community. Successful *apêtê* are dependent not just on knowledge of the immediate properties, but also of long-term successional relationships that change as the forest islands mature and grow. Since many plants are specifically grown to attract useful animals, the complexity of the management problem greatly increases: *apêtê* are managed both as agroforestry units and game reserves. These complexities are not readily visible to those unfamiliar with Kayapó landscapes.

Sacred groves are one of the most common types of cultural landscapes (Laird 1999) and some, like the 'dragon hills' of Yunan Province, China, are kept intact because of their sacred nature (Pei Sheng-Ji 1999). Likewise, Ghjanan groves are linked to burial ground and spirits of the ancestors that protect the forests that surround them (Falconer 1999). Sacred groves in India are extensive and well-known in the literature (Bharucha 1999; Vartak and Gadgil 1981).

Wells and springs are also frequently considered as holy and the areas around them specially protected from disturbance. Wellsprings, for example, are the 'soul of the Hopi people, representing their very identity' (Whitely and Masyesva 1998). Oases too can be sacred places for people like the Maasai and Fulani pastoralists, whose lives during severe droughts literally depend upon these protected areas (Chambers 1999). UNESCO has actually proposed an environmental conservation strategy based on preservation of sacred groves and holy places.

A failure to recognize anthropogenic (human-modified) landscapes has blinded outsiders to the management practices of indigenous peoples and local communities. Many so-called 'pristine' landscapes are in fact *cultural landscapes*, either created by humans or modified by human activity (such as natural forest management, cultivation, and the use of fire).

This is more than mere semantics. 'Wild' and 'wilderness' imply that these landscapes and resources are the result of 'nature' and as such, have no owners—they are thereby considered 'common heritage'. This has come to mean that local communities have no tenurial or ownership rights, and, thus, their lands, territories, and resources are 'free' to others just for the taking. This is why indigenous peoples have come to oppose the use of 'wilderness' and 'wild' to refer to the regions in which they now live or once lived.

This is poignantly expressed in an Aboriginal resolution from the 1995 Ecopolitics IX Conference, Darwin, Australia (Northern Land Council 1996):

The term 'wilderness' as it is popularly used, and related concepts as 'wild resources', 'wild foods', etc. [are unacceptable]. These terms have connotations of terra nullius [empty or unowned land and resources] and, as such, all concerned people and organizations should look for alternative terminology which does not exclude indigenous history and meaning.

Cultural landscapes and their links to conservation of biological diversity are now recognized under the 1972 UNESCO Convention Concerning the Protection of the World Cultural and Natural Heritage ('The World Heritage Convention'). A new category of World Heritage Site, the 'Cultural Landscape', recognizes 'the complex interrelationships between man and nature in the construction, formation and evolution of landscapes'. The first cultural landscape World Heritage Site was Tongariro National Park, a sacred region for the Maori people of New Zealand that was included in the World Heritage List because of its importance in Maori beliefs.

THE CONVENTION ON BIOLOGICAL DIVERSITY

One of the major international initiatives to 'enhance and protect' indigenous and local communities is the Convention on Biological Diversity (CBD), which was opened for signature during the United Nations Conference on Conservation and Development (UNCED) in Rio de Janeiro in 1992. It should be emphasized that the CBD is considered by indigenous peoples to be a sovereignty grab by nation-states over all biological and ecological resources. This is despite the lofty objectives proclaimed in Article 1:

the conservation of biological diversity, the sustainable use of its components and the fair and equitable sharing of the benefits arising out of the utilization of genetic resources, including by appropriate access to genetic resources and by appropriate transfer of relevant technologies, taking into account all rights over those resources and technologies, and by appropriate funding.

'Rights' refers only to the sovereign rights of states. Similarly the beneficiaries of equitable sharing are apparently the contracting parties (the nation-states that ratify the CBD), not individuals or communities. However, Article 8(j) does require that Contracting Parties:

Subject to its national legislation, respect, preserve and maintain knowledge, innovations and practices of indigenous and local communities embodying traditional lifestyles relevant for the conservation and sustainable use of biological diversity and promote the wider application with the approval and involvement of the holders of such knowledge, innovations and practices and encourage the equitable sharing of the benefits arising from the utilization of such knowledge, innovations and practices.

While indigenous peoples might be flattered with the recognition of their relevance to *in situ* conservation, they are hardly convinced that the governments that have tried so hard to destroy them and their habitats are now suddenly going to zealously defend their rights. They are also not convinced that—given their disastrous experiences in the past—any 'equitable sharing' will ever trickle down to the source of both the knowledge and resource, i.e., their communities. Indigenous leaders are both frustrated and angry that while countries do little to protect their interests or guarantee even their most basic rights, they are none the less now anxious to claim sovereignty over even local knowledge systems.

And how will this 'protection' now take place? Intellectual property rights (IPRs) are assumed by the CBD to be the principal mechanisms to provide 'equitable sharing', but IPRs are problematic for developing countries in general—and indigenous, traditional and local communities in particular—for the following reasons:

(i) IPRs are intended to benefit society through the granting of exclusive rights to 'natural' and 'juridical' persons or 'creative individuals', not collective entities such as indigenous peoples. A group of lawyers, academics and activists in the Bellagio Declaration on IPRs summed up the situation:

Contemporary intellectual property law is constructed around the notion of the author as an individual, solitary and original creator, and it is for this figure that its protections are reserved. Those who do not fit this model—custodians of tribal culture and medical knowledge, collectives practising traditional artistic and musical forms, or peasant cultivators of valuable seed varieties, for example—are denied intellectual property protection.

(ii) IPRs cannot protect information that does not result from a specific historic act of 'discovery'. Indigenous knowledge is transgenerational and communally shared. Knowledge may come from ancestor spirits, vision quests, or orally transmitted lineage groups. It is considered to be in the 'public domain' and, therefore, unprotectable.

(iii) IPRs cannot accommodate complex non-western systems of ownership, tenure, and access. IPR law assigns authorship of a song to a writer or publishing company that can record or publish as it sees fit. Indigenous singers, however, may attribute songs to the creator spirit and elders may reserve the right to prohibit its performance, or to limit it to certain occasions and to restricted audiences.

(iv) IPRs serve to stimulate commercialization and distribution, whereas indigenous concerns may be primarily to prohibit commercialization and to restrict use and distribution. As a 1994 COICA (Coordinating Group of the Indigenous Peoples of the Amazon Basin) statement puts it:

> For members of indigenous peoples, knowledge and determination of the use of resources are collective and inter-generational. No indigenous population, whether of individuals or communities, nor the government, can sell or transfer ownership of resources which are the property of the people and which each generation has an obligation to safeguard for the next.

(v) IPRs recognize only market economic values, failing to consider spiritual, aesthetic, or cultural—or even local economic—values. Information or objects may have their greatest value to indigenous peoples because of their ties with cultural identity and symbolic unity.

(vi) IPRs are subject to manipulation by economic interests that wield political power. Sui generis protection has been obtained for semi-conductor chips and 'literary works' generated by computers (Cornish 1993), whereas indigenous peoples have insufficient power to protect even their most sacred plants, places, songs, art, or artefacts.

(vii) IPRs are expensive, complicated, and time-consuming to obtain, and even more difficult to defend.

There are good reasons why indigenous peoples are worried that intellectual property rights cannot protect their knowledge and resources. Take for example, the three patent applications that were made for human cell lines developed from blood 'donated' by indigenous peoples, including one from a member of a recently contacted group of hunter-cultivators in New Guinea, another from the Solomon Islands, and a third from the Guaymi Indians of Panama (Posey and Dutfield 1996: 25–7). The patent applicant in each case is the US National Institute of Health, with the government scientists involved in the project named as *inventors*.

Indigenous peoples in Latin America became acutely aware of how their plants were being patented when *ayahuasca*, a sacred, dream-inducing medicinal drink commonly used by Amazonian Peoples of Ecuador, Colombia and Brazil, was patented by a US scientist/entrepreneur. At the request of indigenous peoples from Ecuador and Colombia—and supported by incredible world-wide pressure—the United States Patents Office revoked the *ayahuasca* patent in November 1999.

In another strange case, a US-based company, POD-NERS, L.L.C, is suing Mexican bean exporters, charging that the Mexican beans (*Phaseolus vulgaris*) they are selling in the US infringe POD-NERS' US patent on a yellow-coloured bean variety. It is not surprising that the Mexican beans are strikingly similar to POD-NER's patented bean: POD-NERS' proprietary bean, 'Enola', originates from the highly popular 'Azufrado' or 'Mayocoba' bean seeds the company's president acquired from Mexican peasant farmers in 1994. The Mexican yellow beans have been grown in Mexico for centuries, developed by generations of Mexican farmers and more recently by Mexican plant breeders.

These examples illustrate why indigenous communities are less than enthusiastic about and trustful of scientists. They also explain why patents (the focus of IPR debates) have become a new war-cry for indigenous rights.

In a now famous declaration from a UNDP Consultation on the Protection and Conservation of Indigenous Knowledge, organized by indigenous groups from Bolivia and COICA at Santa Cruz de la Sierra in September 1994, indigenous leaders declared a moratorium on all research and bioprospecting until appropriate protection measures are in place (see Posey and Dutfield 1996). The threat of a moratorium is unnerving, since scientists and research institutions are increasingly dependent upon the private sector for their livelihoods. This means the fruits of their labours are subject to commercial exploitation, or indeed, are now designed for that purpose (Posey 1995). It is often hard for scientists themselves to know when they must wear the hat of their patrons versus the mantle of their scientific discipline. From the indigenous perspective, they are all the same. This means that negotiating access by scientists to indigenous and local communities—whether for bioprospecting or scientific purposes—may take considerable time and energy and has become a profoundly political act (Posey, Dutfield and Plenderleith 1995).

The private sector and scientific interests are eager that the CBD resolve these dilemmas to become an international vehicle for clarification of the terms of access for and transfer of genetic resources and appropriate technologies. Indeed, the CBD has advanced considerably towards the development of guidelines and principles for *sui generis* options to existing IPRs. The Third Conference of the Parties (COP-III) of the CBD, held in Buenos Aires in 1996, discussed Article 8(j) and intellectual property rights and agreed to 'develop national legislation and corresponding strategies for the implementation of Article 8(j) in consultation with representatives of their indigenous and local communities' (Decision III/14).

An inter-sessional Workshop on Traditional Knowledge and Bio-diversity was held in Madrid in November 1997, and proposed to COP-IV that a 'participatory mechanism' be established to review legal elements related to benefit-sharing and traditional cultural practices for conservation and sustainable use. COP-IV (Decision IV/8) agreed to establish a 'regionally balanced panel of experts' to develop a 'common understanding of basic concepts and to explore all options for access and benefit-sharing on mutually agreed terms including principles, guidelines, and codes of best practices for access and benefit-sharing arrangements'.

Decision IV/9 on 'Implementation of Article *8(j)* and Related Provisions' specifically recognized the 'importance of making intellectual property-related provisions of the Convention on Biological Diversity and provisions of international agreements relating to intellectual property mutually supportive, and the desirability of undertaking further co-operation and consultation with the World Intellectual Property Organization'. The decision also agreed to establish an *ad hoc* open-ended inter-sessional working group to address IPR and issues related to Article 8(j). The working group has now embraced a work plan that includes investigation of options for *sui generis* protection for traditional knowledge, innovations, and practices, as well as genetic resources for indigenous and local communities.

Although international efforts to recognize indigenous, traditional and local communities are welcome and positive, they are pitted against enormous economic and market forces that propel globalization of trade. Critiques of globalization are numerous and point to at least two major shortcomings: (i) value is imputed to information and resources only when they enter external markets; and (ii) expenditures do not reflect actual environmental and social costs (see Strong, this volume). This means that existing values recognized by local communities are ignored, despite knowledge that local biodiversity provides essential elements for survival (food, shelter, medicine, etc.). It also means that the knowledge and managed resources of indigenous and traditional peoples are ascribed no value and assumed to be free for the taking. This has been called 'intellectual *terra nullius*' after the concept (empty land) that allowed colonial powers to expropriate 'discovered' land for their empires. Corporations and states still defend this morally vacuous concept because it facilitates the 'bio-piracy' of local folk varieties of crops, traditional medicines, and useful species.

Scientists have been accomplices to such raids by publishing data they know will be catapulted into the public domain and gleaned by 'bio-prospectors' seeking new products. They have also perpetuated the 'intellectual *terra nullius*' concept by declaring useful local plants as 'wild' and entire ecosystems as 'wildernesses', often despite knowing that these have been moulded, managed, and protected by human populations for millennia. It is also common for scientists to declare areas and resources 'wild' through ignorance—or negligence—without even basic investigations into archaeological or historical records, or to actual human management practices. The result is to declare the biodiversity of a site as 'natural', thereby transferring it to the public domain. Once public, communities are stripped of all rights to their traditional resources.

It is only fair to say that intellectual property rights have become major issues not only in international political debates, but also within academic and research institutions. This interest may be more because of enlightened self-interest than it is to investigate and implement mechanisms that will enhance and protect the knowledge and resources of local and indigenous communities.

STEPS IN THE RIGHT DIRECTION

Scientific societies, research institutions, governments and corporations have begun to develop Codes of Ethics and Standards of Practice to provide a moral compass for collaboration with indigenous peoples. The most far-reaching of these is that of the International Society for Ethnobiology (see http://users.ox.ac.uk/~wgtrr/isecode).

Similar principles have been elaborated by environmental philosophers, ethicists, and eco-theologians. Unfortunately their efforts have often been couched in such rarefied discourses that they have had little impact on the practice of science or on public policy.

There are some important exceptions to this, notably 'deep ecology', which has inspired a militant 'Earth First' movement aimed at extinguishing the anthropocentric view that humans have the right to do as they wish to other life forms. For deep ecologists, 'the *hubris* in asking people "to take responsibility" for the environment is replaced by an invitation to realize the depth of existing ecological relationships' (Golliher 1988). Ingold has long argued for a discourse that avoids anthropocentrism and ethnocentrism, in favour of an 'ontological equality' (Ingold *et al.* 1988). To a large extent, this requires shifting priorities from *instrumental values* (how is biodiversity useful to humans) to *intrinsic values* (all life is valuable whether it is of use to humans or not)—not an easy task in a world dominated by economics and global trade.

'Ecofeminism' has also been instrumental in pointing out how unequal gender and power relations have operated to separate 'nature' from 'spirit', thereby catalysing disrespect for biodiversity and destruction of eco-systems. This emphasis on 'spirit' provides a much-needed bridge between cultures, since 'cosmovisions' are the organizing spiritual and conceptual models used by indigenous and traditional peoples to integrate their society with the world. These cosmovisions are based on the 'sacred bal-ance' of cosmic forces that unite human beings (males and females equally) with all life (again, equally shared).

Many people in industrialized countries are trying to reintegrate the concept of 'Sacred Balance' into a practical 'ethic' of land, biodiversity, and environment. This movement takes its inspiration from Aldo Leopold's (1949) ideas of 'land ethic' and 'environmental citizenship'. There is a *need for* a global ethic formulated around respect for the diversity of cultures and ecosystems (Callicott 1989). It may be that the 'need' is not just the artefact of human psychology and moral reflection, but rather spiritually and psychologically grounded. Some believe that the environmental crisis is rooted in the extreme 'disturbance' of the web of life that is a part of human consciousness (Roszak 1992).

Indeed, a basic precept of ecology itself is that disturbance of one ele-ment of an environmental systems affects all other elements, as well as the whole. It may be conjecture as to how *Homo sapiens* is psychologically affected by the overall loss of biological and cultural diversity, but certain-ly indigenous, traditional and local communities are aware of the negative local affects—and they express their profound concerns in cultural and spiritual terms precisely because they recognize the deep cosmic connect-edness of the disturbance.

CONCLUDING REMARKS

The worrisome lesson from all of this is that the global environmental crisis cannot be solved by technological tampering ('quick fixes') or superficial political measures. For industrialized society to reverse the devastating cycles it has imposed on the planet, it will have to invent an 'ecology' powerful enough to offset deforestation, soil erosion, species extinction, and pollution; find 'sustainable practices' that can harmonize with growth of trade and increased consumption; and, of course, establish a 'global environmental ethic' that is not fragmented by economically powerful institutions.

That may be an impossible task—but there are some viable paths. One of the best options is to re-learn the ecological knowledge and sustainable principles that our society has lost. This can come through listening to the indigenous and traditional peoples of the planet who still know when birds nest, fish migrate, ants swarm, tadpoles develop legs, soils erode, and rare plants seed—and whose cosmovisions manifest the ecologies and ethics of sustainability. As Chief Bepkororoti Paiakan of the Kayapó said: 'We are trying to save the knowledge that the forests and this Planet are alive—to give it back to you who have lost the understanding.'

The Kayapó story of 'The Journey to Become a Shaman' illustrates how cosmic energy lives only when it flows through humans and animals, through colours and sounds, through life—and then only when it is shared and passed on to future generations. Indigenous beliefs are based upon the inextricable link between culture and nature, which are celebrated through place-based knowledge systems that cannot be removed from land, territory or sacred places.

The commodification of nature through globalization of markets has allowed policy-makers and developers to reduce cultural landscapes to real estate, sacred sites to development plots, cultural heritage to tourist trinkets, and spiritual energy of plants and animals into products for biotechnology. IPRs have been a major mechanism for this disturbance of the Sacred Balance. And until the international community can provide some meaningful countermeasures to this onslaught of decontextualization, there is little hope that a global environmental (and social) crisis can be avoided.

If there is hope, it lies with the survival of indigenous peoples like the Kayapó, who have undergone centuries of harsh and devastating conditions and still resist, while generously offering their wisdom to people from societies like ours—that have fragmented almost beyond repair the cosmic connections that link life and the Earth.

REFERENCES

Bharucha, E. (1999). 'Cultural and spiritual values related to the conservation of biodiversity in the sacred groves of the Western Ghats in Maharashtra', in Posey 1999: 382–5.

Callicott, J. B. (1989). *In Defense of the Land Ethic: Essays in Environmental Philosophy*. Albany, NY: State University of New York Press.

Chambers, P. (1999). 'Aquatic and marine biodiversity: Introduction', in Posey 1999, 399–402.

Cornish, W. R. (1993). 'The international relations of intellectual property', *Cambridge Law Journal*, 52(1): 46–63.

Dobkin de Rios, Marlene (1992). *Amazon Healer: The Life and Times of an Urban Shaman.* Bridport: Prism.

Durning, A. T. (1992). *Guardians of the Land: Indigenous Peoples and the Health of the Earth.* Washington, DC: Worldwatch.

Elisabetsky, E. and D. A. Posey (1989). 'Use of contraceptive and related plants by the Kayapó Indians (Brazil)', *Journal of Ethnopharmacology*, 26: 299–316. (Also in Posey 2002.)

Falconer, J. 1999. 'Non-timber forest products in southern Ghana: traditional and cultural forest values', in Posey 1999: 366–70.

Barbira-Freedman, F. (1999). '*Vegetalismo* and the perception of biodiversity: shamanic values in the Peruvian upper Amazon', in Posey 1999: 277–8.

Golliher, J. (1999). 'Ethical, moral and religious concerns: introduction', in Posey 1999: 437–50.

Harrison, K. (1999). 'Spirit, story and medicine: *Sachamama*—an example of the ancient beings of the Amazon rainforest', in Posey 1999: 276.

Ingold, T., D. Riches, and J. Woodburn (eds.) (1988) *Hunters and Gatherers*, Vol 1: *History, Evolution and Social Change*; Vol. 2: *Property, Power and Ideology.* Oxford: Berg.

Laird, S. A. (1999). 'Forests, culture and conservation: introduction', in Posey 1999: 347–58.

Leopold, A. (1949). *A Sand County Almanac and Sketches Here and There.* New York: Oxford University Press.

Martins, H. (1993). 'Hegel, Texas: issues in the philosophy and sociology of technology', in H. Martins (ed.), *Knowledge and Passion: Essays in Honour of John Rex.* London: Tauris, 226–49.

Northern Land Council (1996). *Ecopolitics IX: Perspectives on Indigenous Peoples' Management of Environment Resources.* Darwin: Northern Land Council.

Pei Sheng-Ji (1999). 'The holy hills of the Dai', in Posey 1999: 381.

Posey, D. A., G. Dutfield and K. Plenderleith (1995). 'Collaborative research and intellectual property rights', *Biodiversity and Conservation* 4: 892–902.

Posey, D. A. and G. Dutfield (1996). *Beyond Intellectual Property: Toward Traditional Resource Rights for Indigenous Peoples and Local Communities.* Ottawa: International Development Research Centre.

Posey, D. A., and E. Elisabetsky (1991). 'Conceitos de animais e seus espíritos em relação a doenças e curas entre os indios Kayapó da Aldeia Gorotire', *Boletim do Museu Paraense Emílio Goeldi*, 7(1): 21–36.

Posey, D. A., and W. Overal (eds.) (1990). *Ethnobiology: Implications and Applications. Proceedings of the First International Congress of Ethnobiology*, Volume 1. Belém, Pará: Museu Paraense Emilio Goeldi.

Posey, D. A. (1982). 'The journey to become a shaman: a narrative of sacred transition of the Kayapó Indians of Brazil', *Journal of Latin American Indian Literature*, 7(1): 13–19.

Posey, D. A. (1985). 'Indigenous management of tropical forest ecosystems: the case of the Kayapó indians of the Brazilian Amazon', *Agroforestry Systems* 3(2): 139–58. (Also in Posey 2002: Ch. 18)

Posey, D. A. (1990). 'The science of the Mebengokre', *Orion*, Summer: 16–23. (Also in Posey 2002: Ch. 1)

Posey, D. A. (1995). *Indigenous Peoples and Traditional Resource Rights: A Basis for Equitable Relationships?* Oxford: Green College Centre for Environmental Policy and Understanding. (Also as Chapter 16 in Posey, D. A. (forthcoming). *Indigenous Knowledge and Ethics*. London and New York: Routledge.)

Posey, D. A. (1997). 'The Kayapó', in *Indigenous Peoples and Sustainability: Cases and Actions.* IUCN Inter-Commission Task Force on Indigenous Peoples. Utrecht: IUCN and International Books, 240–54.

Posey, D. A. (1999). *Cultural and Spiritual Values of Biodiversity.* Nairobi: Intermediate Technology Publications/United Nations Environment Programme.

Posey, D. A. (2002). *Kayapó Ethnoecology and Culture* (ed. K. Plenderleith). London and New York: Routledge.

Roszak, T. (1992). *The Voice of the Earth.* New York: Simon & Schuster.

Strathern, M. (1996). 'Potential property: intellectual rights and property in persons', *Social Anthropology* 4(1): 17–32.

Sultan, R., D. Craig and H. Ross (1997). 'Aboriginal joint management of Australian national parks: Uluru-kata Tjuta', in D. A. Posey and G. Dutfield (eds.) *Indigenous Peoples and Sustainability: Cases and Actions.* Utrecht: IUCN and International Books.

UNESCO (1993). *Amendment to the Draft Programme and Budget for 1994–1995 (27 C/5), Item 5 of the Provisional Agenda* (27 C/DR.321). Paris: UNESCO.

Vartak, V. D. and M. Gadgil (1981). 'Studies on sacred groves along the Western Ghats from Maharashtra and Goa: role of beliefs and folklore', in S. K. Jain (ed.), *Glimpses of Indian Ethnobotany.* Delhi: OUP and IBH Publishing, 272–8.

Whiteley, P. and V. Masayesva (1999). '*Paavahu* and *Paanaqso'a*: the wellsprings of life and the slurry of death', in Posey 1999: 403–6.

9

The 'Wild', the Market, and the Native: Indigenous People Face New Forms of Global Colonization

Marcia Langton

INDIGENOUS and traditional peoples world-wide are facing a crisis, one that supersedes that inflicted on indigenous peoples during the imperial age. Just as in the last 500 years, imperialism caused the encapsulation of indigenous societies within the new settler nation-states and their subjection to colonial political formations, loss of territory and jurisdiction, so have the globalizing market and the post-industrial/technological complex brought about another phase of profound change for these societies. The further encapsulation of indigenous societies by the global complex, to which nation-state formations are themselves subservient, has resulted in continuing loss of territory as a result of large-scale developments, urban postcolonial population expansion, and ongoing colonization of the natural world by the market. This last point is illustrated, for example, by the bioprospecting and patenting of life forms and biota by new genetic and chemical engineering industries (see Posey, this volume). Coincidental with the new colonization is the crisis of biodiversity loss; a critical issue for indigenous peoples, particularly hunting and gathering societies. The massive loss of biota through extinction events, loss of territory and species habitats, and environmental degradation, together with conservationist limitation of indigenous harvesting, constitute significant threats to indigenous ways of life.

While aboriginal rights to wildlife are restricted to 'non-commercial' use, the pressures increase for indigenous peoples to forge unique economic niches to maintain their ways of life. Of particular importance is the vexed issue of aboriginal entitlements to commercial benefits from the utilization of wildlife arising both from developing standards of traditional resource rights and from customary proprietary interests.

IMPACT OF THE GLOBAL MARKET ON THE
INDIGENOUS WORLD

The new threats to indigenous life-ways in the era of the globalizing market have been brought about by the increasing commodification of features of the natural world, putting at risk the very survival of ancient societies that are directly dependent on the state of their natural environment. For instance, already in June 1978, Inupiat leader Eben Hopson,[1] then founding Chairman of the Inuit Circumpolar Conference and spokesperson for the Alaska Whaling Commission, appealed to the London press corps for understanding and support in the legal recognition of Inuit rights: 'We Inuit are hunters. There aren't many subsistence hunting societies left in the world, but our Inuit circumpolar community is one of them.'

The dilemma for indigenous peoples is also a political one, especially for those groups encapsulated by settler states that oppose developing standards of rights for indigenous peoples. As well as the opposition by some governments seeking to appropriate indigenous lands and resources, conservationist organizations resist compromise on land use issues because they believe that global biodiversity preservation goals take precedence over the needs of local people. In some instances, because of conflict between indigenous and conservationist groups, common biodiversity conservation goals, in locations where development projects have threatened environmental values, have not been achieved. In their feasibility study in the Torres Strait Islands region, Dews *et al.* (1997: 48) explain that while indigenous concerns are often pressing and immediate, 'biodiversity defenders look to the distant future'. Of critical relevance here is their conclusion: ' in the final analysis, property rights and especially the management of common property resources, may become the focal issue for both camps'.

A number of cases of the suppression, or attempted suppression, of indigenous economic activity provide evidence of environmental racism. Conservationist lobbying at the International Whaling Commission to prevent Inuit hunting of the Bowhead, Narwhal and Beluga whales is one infamous case among many.[2] By targeting small-scale indigenous groups

---

[1] Eben Hopson, 1922–1980, was an Inupiat (Northern Eskimo) leader, founder of the North Slope Borough (a county-like home rule municipal government serving the people of Alaska's vast 86,000-square mile Arctic Slope between Pt. Hope and the border of the Yukon Territory) and founder of the Inuit Circumpolar Conference. See *Hopson's Address to the London Press Corps* 23 June 1978 at URL: http://www.buchholdt.com/EbenHopson/papers/1978/London.html

[2] See the account by Eben Hopson in *Hopson's Address to the London Press Corps* 23 June 1978 at URL: http://www.buchholdt.com/EbenHopson/papers/1978/London.html and

in their campaigns against national and multinational environmental violations, conservation organizations privilege global commercialization of the natural world over ancient economic systems in their increasing demands for the suppression of traditional forms of wildlife exploitation. Thus, subsequent to the deteriorating environmental circumstances of small-scale hunting and gathering peoples is the further limitation of their territorial base and traditional economic means by environmental racism. The high dependence of marginalized native peoples on wildlife resources for basic subsistence needs is typically ignored by conservationists whose goal of biodiversity conservation is not based on local knowledge of particular small-scale societies that are co-located with species targeted by conservation campaigns. Little regard is paid to the actual impacts of local populations and, instead, highly emotive claims are made about the presumed threats without substantial or rigorous scientific research to support such claims. With their minimal and often inaccurate understanding of indigenous societies, environmental scientists, planners and managers have the potential to cause great harm to native peoples. Capacity-building and developing enterprise and investment strategies may well contribute to conservation goals more directly than any purely conservationist strategy aimed at national goals. Indigenous societies face increasing hardships as governments, conservation campaigners and the private sector further marginalize them. Furze, de Lacey and Birckhead (1996:3), referring to a range of international case studies, make the point that 'many protected areas are at risk because of the hardship they place on local communities. The protection of biodiversity may therefore be seen to be one of the most pressing issues in development.'

With the recognition that conservation often fails to achieve its goals when local people are unsupportive, or are not meaningful partners, the question of local participation is now firmly on international conservation and sustainable development agendas. As a result, many people involved in the conservation, development and academic communities, as well as local people themselves, are involved in the search for sustainable futures.

Posey and Duttfield (1996) have offered comprehensive accounts of the nature of the rights of local traditional peoples in resources and cultural and intellectual property, and protection of such rights in the context of sustainable traditional use of resources. They observe that environmental concerns increasingly focus on the roles of indigenous peoples and local communities in enhancing and maintaining biological diversity. Detailing

Goodman, D., 'Land claim agreements and the management of whaling in the Canadian Arctic', *Proceedings 11th. International Symposium on Peoples and Cultures of the North.* Hokkaido Museum of Northern Peoples. Abashiri, Japan. 1996, at URL: http://www. highnorth.no/Library/Policies/National/la-cl-ag.htm the provisions of each of the relevant conventions, statements and case law that impact on traditional peoples, they provide a wealth of knowledge for local groups wanting to pursue their rights. They must do so in relation to an absence of effective measures. For instance, as Posey observes, 'The Convention on Biological Diversity (CBD) does not provide specific mechanisms to protect the rights of indigenous peoples and local communities to their genetic materials, knowledge and technologies' (1996: xiii). As he points out, however, the Convention does recognize that 'knowledge, innovations and practices of indigenous and local communities embodying traditional lifestyles' are central to successful *in situ* conservation. Moreover, the fundamental importance of benefit-sharing and compensation for the peoples and communities providing traditional knowledge, innovations and practices is also acknowledged. Posey's approach is to present the concept of traditional resource rights 'to guide the development of *sui generis* systems, premised on human rights principles (1996: xiii). The concept of traditional resource rights, he explains, is a process and a framework to develop multiple, locally appropriate systems and 'solutions' that reflect the diversity of contexts where *sui generis* systems are required.

The coincidence of the remnant indigenous territories and high biodiversity values, the globalizing market, and the growing recognition of resource rights for traditional peoples requires special attention as a problem of biodiversity maintenance. This is evident in Australia, where indigenous societies have lost 85 per cent of their traditional land base since British colonizers arrived in 1788. The remaining 15 per cent of the Australian landmass under various forms of title owned by Aboriginal groups is an exemplary locus of this predicament.

The impact of globalization on the indigenous world brings with its threats and benefits a profound contradiction: the global market itself poses the end of ancient ways of human life and yet at the same time offers opportunities for accommodating these life-ways to the new market forces with benefits for all of human society. The central benefit is the maintenance of biodiversity typical of the last 10,000 years of human history and sustained throughout the imperial and industrial ages by local indigenous peoples. As the imperative for further commercialization of the natural world, by, for instance, wildlife harvesting, intrudes into the indigenous domains,[3] there are opportunities for rapidly adapting indigenous societies

[3] The term 'indigenous domain' is used to refer to indigenous governance of territory, including title under settler or indigenous legal systems. This would include: land and water whether owned under Australian title or not, and in the latter case, whether or not under claim under native title or other legislation; and, land and water under contemporary forms of indigenous governance, including local customary forms of governance, representative bodies, community councils, etc.

to maintain their fundamental ideas about, and relationships with, the natural world while exploring what may be offered by the application of ecologically sustainable development practices in their territories.

THE ROLE OF INDIGENOUS PEOPLE IN BIODIVERSITY CONSERVATION

In spite of the unsubstantiated claims of some conservationist organizations, there is increasing recognition of the role of indigenous cultures in supporting biodiversity. For example, Nietschmann (1992: 7) made this point eloquently:

The vast majority of the world's biological diversity is not in gene banks, zoos, national parks, or protected areas. Most biological diversity is in landscapes and seascapes inhabited and used by local peoples, mostly indigenous, whose great collective accomplishment is to have conserved the great variety of remaining life forms, using culture, the most powerful and valuable human resource, to do so.

The critical role of indigenous peoples in biodiversity conservation is no less the case in Australia. Indigenous involvement is essential to the Australian project of land, water and biodiversity conservation for a number of reasons. Land and water subject to indigenous ownership and governance constitutes a significant proportion of the Australian continent. Those lands and waters which constitute most of that area are not subject to high density settlement, degradation of natural values by industries such as agriculture, forestry, fishing, pastoralism and tourism, and are high-integrity areas both in terms of natural and cultural values. Much of the lands and waters within the indigenous domain remain subject to indigenous management systems that have persisted since the late Pleistocene, and include, for instance, the wet tropics and the wet-dry tropics, parts of which are listed as World Heritage Areas and other World Conservation Union categories. In these regions, there have been few, or no, extinctions of native fauna and flora. This contrasts starkly with the southern settled areas of Australia where the majority of extinctions have occurred, placing the nation amongst the worst offenders, despite the small population and relatively short record of colonial settlement.

Within the indigenous domain, there are indigenous systems of governance, with significance for the conservation challenges of this area. These are discussed further below. One of the important aspects of indigenous governance is the existence of vast indigenous knowledge systems based on the very long periods of living on the continent (presently understood to exceed 40,000 years) and the intimacy of indigenous social life with the physical world, the biota, and its systems. The loss of these knowledge systems would constitute an irretrievable loss to human cultural diversity and therefore to our capacity to understand human relationships with the world—relationships on which our search for sustainable futures depends.

In Australia, the extant territory within the contemporary indigenous domain—especially the large land and marine estates remote from non-urban areas—is the result of a colonial history that, especially over the first 150 years following invasion, favoured occupation of coastal regions in the south and east of the continent. Non-Aboriginal land use in Australia proceeded from earliest colonial times by radically altering extant environments, through extensive land clearing, water capture and other means. The British settlers perceived their new environments as harsh and inhospitable and they actively supplanted these 'wild', uncultivated lands with familiar European land use and management systems, which they believed they could control, regardless of whether or not these imported management regimes were suitable to local conditions. As a result, settlers engaged in wide-scale clearing of vegetation, suppression of fire, development of irrigation systems, widespread use of pesticides and the attempted eradication of native animals such as dingoes. Spinks (personal communication) reports that 76 per cent of Australia's 20,000 or so species of plants are now extinct, while some 5,000 others are considered to be rare or threatened (see also Spinks 1999). Significant proportions of native mammals, reptiles, amphibians, birds, freshwater fish and marsupials are also threatened or extinct. Land and water resources have been degraded: agricultural land is plagued by salination, caused by clearing and irrigation, while fish and other aquatic life are at risk in inland waterways from the effects of toxic algae, exotic competitors, inbreeding, and through the removal or degradation of some of their natural habitats. Introduced agricultural regimes were ill-suited to the arid rangelands and deserts that cover most of Australia's landmass. Therefore, with some exceptions, the indigenous domain has tended to be concentrated in desert and wetland environments of little apparent use to the colonizers.

The biological integrity of the indigenous domain has suffered considerably less than that of the lands which have been radically altered to suit the imported management systems and understandings of the settler society. Of course, this pattern of remnant indigenous territory being located on the remote periphery of settler states is a world-wide phenomenon and similar patterns of environmental degradation in the non-indigenous domains are evident in countries other than Australia. The indigenous knowledge systems that have shaped and governed the Australian continent and its natural systems survive in many areas. It is in those areas of Australia—where high levels of biological integrity coincide with indigenous customary governance and knowledge systems—that opportunities exist to maintain that biological integrity through a strategic process that includes indigenous management systems.

With the exception of relatively small-scale mining operations and low capital settler pastoralism highly dependent on largely unpaid indigenous labour, it was not until the expansion of large-scale resource extraction from the 1950s that this indigenous domain came under significant threat. This expansion into indigenous lands by large-scale extractive industries, together with substantial technological changes within the pastoral industry, has coincided with an upsurge in assertiveness of re-politicized indigenous peoples and moves away from protectionism and assimilationism that previously characterized Australian colonialism. One of the consequences of this history has been the development in more recent times of relationships between indigenous and non-indigenous people in land, sea and resource management, based on an acknowledgement of the special knowledge and practices that the indigenous people bring to the task.

Few people seriously doubt any longer that Aboriginal people *manage* their lands and seas. Aboriginal management of their land and sea estates is understood as being based upon their detailed knowledge of all its features. Much of that knowledge is embedded in religious beliefs and practices, and is inextricably linked to the system of land tenure. The question as to whether the management is explicit and principled, or merely a consequence of practices recognized *post facto*, is, however, still sometimes raised.

James Kohen, an archaeologist, in his book *Aboriginal Environmental Impacts* (1996: 125), makes a distinction between management and exploitation: 'Essentially, management involves the utilization of the landscape without any long-term deterioration, whereas exploitation involves long-term degradation to the detriment of the environment.' He identifies two main interrelated factors that determine whether land use practices can be defined as management or exploitation. The first is the nature of the land-use strategy and the second is the human population density. Both of these factors may seem intuitively obvious, but they need to be justified because of the implications for our understanding of traditional and contemporary Aboriginal societies and the nature of their impact on the environment. Once land management practices were adopted by early human populations on the Australian continent to increase the productivity of the landscape, there were pressures on their communities to maintain the environments they had created in order to feed the growing population. The environment that confronted Europeans in 1788 was certainly one that was managed. The biogeographical history of Australia determined the range of plant and animal species that would occur within the region, but, to some extent, the balance and distribution of species had been altered, not only by climate change, but also by Aboriginal impacts. Most significant of these was the human use of fire as a management tool in a fire-prone continent, resulting in seasonal mosaic patterns across landscapes that prevented destructive, hot wildfires.

Such Holocene-period land management practices continue in the indigenous domain today and Aboriginal leaders advocate that environmental protection and wildlife management depend on the protection of indigenous cultural values and lifestyles because of the co-dependency of the natural world and indigenous use and management. Aboriginal strategies include local and regional multiple-use management planning for sustainable terrestrial, marine and coastal resources. To achieve conservation objectives, traditional practices alone are no match for the rapid population and development of indigenous territories by the settler state. Indigenous people and their local and regional bodies require collaborative relationships with other individuals and organizations in order to meet particular, identified challenges. Success in such collaboration depends on highly qualified and experienced collaborators with a high level of commitment to the integrity of indigenous laws.

As an example, we can look at strategies needed to control outbreaks of invasive weeds like weeds *Mimosa pigra* and *Salvinia*. Because mechanical and chemical controls are limited in their capacity to prevent such outbreaks, regional multiple land-use planning and inter-agency co-ordination and sharing of resources are required for long-term control. Indigenous people have developed regional plans, particularly at the catchment level, in coastal northern Australia. Examples of such exercises include the projects of the Dhimurru Land Management Corporation in north-east Arnhem Land, the Arafura Catchment Management Plan in central Arnhem Land, and the Alice–Mitchell Basin management plan developed by the Kowanyama community in western Cape York Peninsula.

It is also in these biodiversity-rich areas of Australia that Australian governments are permitting commercial harvesting of wildlife. A number of large and small corporations are presently carrying out bioprospecting activities for commercial gain on indigenous land in Australia. While some of these activities are subject to satisfactory agreements, most are not. Commercial utilization of wildlife is also gaining increasing support from governments that have established licence regimes for commercial harvesters. Except where indigenous people have established their own wildlife harvesting enterprises or negotiated agreements with bioprospecting companies, they receive no benefits from the industry. Their involvement in any capacity is minimal and the notion that indigenous groups may have customary proprietary interests in these wild resources has not been considered. Such appropriation of natural resources from the indigenous domain is a new form of dispossession.

ARGUMENTS ABOUT SUSTAINABILITY AND INDIGENOUS USE OF WILDLIFE

Indigenous people are subjected to highly political demands from an uninformed public to cease customary hunting and gathering based on conjecture regarding indigenous contributions to population declines of some species, such as dugong and turtle. That such declines are more likely to be attributed to large-scale commercial, agricultural and industrial activities (particularly pollution of seabed grasses by run-off of agricultural chemicals) than to small-scale customary use has only recently become the subject of research in plant and animal population studies. Emotive public campaigns (notably by extremist animal rights lobby groups) threaten legislative and structural reforms necessary to develop viable enterprises and they can only be countered by sound scientific evidence as to the sustainable use of any particular species.

Scientific and government responses to the use of wildlife by indigenous peoples and popular concern over its possible impact on conservation of wildlife have led to demands for planning and regulation. Such regulation and planning severely limit Aboriginal hunting in Australia, particularly when indigenous hunting and gathering practices have been targeted as being the principle threat to endangered species. A frequent specific objection is that traditional hunters should not be permitted to use modern technology such as vehicles and guns. However, such views can be best understood as settler state cultural hangovers from a frontier society that almost achieved the extinction of Aboriginal peoples on the Australian continent. The primitivist conception of Aboriginal life as a remnant 'Stone Age' is a powerful cultural force in Australian life and is typically expressed in highly contradictory ways. For instance, on the one hand, there is the insistent demand that Aboriginal people should assimilate (or 'become like white people') according to the premise that white settler ways of life are better. On the other hand, the use of vehicles or guns by Aboriginal people is highly unpopular in the electorate because of the clash with the primitivist ideals that Aboriginal people are required to fulfil. The result is that most governments in Australia have effectively banned traditional hunting and gathering.

Conservationist objections to Aboriginal life, when rationally analysed, are also cultural in the sense that the objections are often aesthetic in

nature, inferring a contempt for 'distasteful' aspects of Aboriginal economic life, particularly hunting practices. The contribution of such practices to conservation aims is consequently ignored. A good example of this
cultural blindness is a report prepared for the Australian Bureau of
Resource Sciences by Bomford and Caughley (1996). The stated aim of this
work was to assess 'the appropriateness of planned wildlife use in terms of
benefits to Aboriginal peoples and Torres Strait Islanders' and 'the sustainability of wildlife use, and of the land, waters and other components of
the natural systems they are part of'. The authors propose various forms of
social engineering in order to achieve sustainable levels of wildlife resource
use, as defined by environmental managers. The euphemistic use of language to discuss highly contentious issues such as Aboriginal use of fire-
arms is exemplified in the following recommendation: 'A process to
address community concerns over the use of modern technology in traditional hunting practices and a recognition and integration of indigenous
and non-indigenous cultural perceptions and aspirations concerning the
sustainability of indigenous wildlife use . . .' (ibid.: 1).

The authors further speculate about 'possible overexploitation of
resources through subsistence hunting due to the loss of traditional regulatory mechanisms caused by societal changes and the interface of this with
cash-based economies'. Contrary to all available rigorous research in the
field, these environmental 'experts' recommend for indigenous people 'an
analysis of the need for access to a cash income to underwrite an indigenous subsistence lifestyle'. Yet despite offering uninformed speculation
about Aboriginal use of guns and the impact of this on biota, the authors
admit that there is a need for 'more data on the ecological factors that affect
the sustainability of wildlife harvests. Data on many wildlife species is
lacking and is required to fit complex harvest models' (ibid.: 2). The
authors also admit that there is a need for: 'Case studies where wildlife use
is an important component of the culture of Australian indigenous peoples. This includes the need for data on harvesting and its relevance to the
communities concerned, as well as the legal constraints in the management
of the resource' (ibid.).

The report advocates that government agencies should respond to
requests by indigenous peoples for increased funding to manage their
natural resources by considering, as part their decision-making processes,
'a complex array of scientific, economic and social issues'. The recommendations of this report fail to acknowledge traditional resource rights and
ignore indigenous rights in favour of conservation objectives for wildlife
protection without regard to indigenous cultural relationships with, and
dependence on, 'wildlife'. In studies such as this, indigenous people are
marginalized to the extent that their own aspirations for their futures are

diminished. It is assumed in this report, and many others like it, that settler society aspirations should take precedence over all other life-ways. Thus the authors believe it is sufficient to emphasize the need for protocols for consultations with indigenous people as if they were mere 'stakeholders' like other settler state stakeholders in the wildlife use planning processes.

At the same time commercial exploitation of wild plant and animal products is widespread in Australia, in industries such as: commercial fishing; pharmaceutical bioprospecting; gardening and horticultural enterprises; edible plant and animal marketing; skin, hide and other animal product marketing; the pet food industry; the timber and sylviculture industries. The indigenous participation in these industries is minuscule. Moreover, government-sponsored culling of native species such as kangaroos, emus and koalas goes without comment. Such inconsistencies between the actual situation and public perceptions raise the problem of environmental racism. I draw attention to this issue because of its contribution to perpetuating social and economic inequity and injustice for indigenous peoples.

In contrast to the speculation of such quasi-scientific reports as that commissioned by the Bureau of Resource Sciences, the policy and research programmes in which indigenous people have played a substantial role have produced quite different outcomes—outcomes that present the possibility of a viable future for indigenous life-ways. For example, in response to the Convention on Biological Diversity 1992, ratified by Australia in 1993, the Australian Government consulted Aboriginal representatives in producing the *National Strategy for the Conservation of Australia's Biological Diversity* (1996). This *National Strategy* recommends a framework in which governments, industry, community groups and individual landowners can work cooperatively to 'bridge the gap between current efforts and the effective identification, conservation and management of Australia's biological diversity'. The report acknowledges that Australian indigenous cultures 'maintain a lively interest in, practical knowledge of, and concern for the wellbeing of the land and natural systems'. Moreover, the *Strategy* recognizes that 'The maintenance of biological diversity . . . is a cornerstone of the wellbeing, identity, cultural heritage and economy of Aboriginal and Torres Strait Islander communities.'

Objective 1.8 of the *National Strategy* is the recognition and maintenance of 'the contribution of the ethnobiological knowledge of Australia's indigenous peoples to the conservation of Australia's biological diversity'. The *Strategy* also acknowledges that indigenous law and cosmology establish intimate associations between land, people and other species and ensure the transmission of this knowledge across the generations. While the *Strategy* notes that traditional Aboriginal and Torres Strait Islander management practices have already proved significant for the maintenance of biodiversity and should be incorporated into mainstream management programmes where appropriate, it also cautions that access to this specialist knowledge is not guaranteed. 'Although Aboriginal and Torres Strait Islander peoples may be willing to share some of their cultural knowledge, aspects of that knowledge may be privileged and may not be available to the public domain.'

The *Strategy* recommends that governments provide resources for the conservation of traditional biological knowledge through cooperative ethnobiological programmes. It further proposes that because Aboriginal and Torres Strait Islander peoples have access to accurate information about biological diversity, they should be involved in research programmes relevant to the biological diversity and management of the lands and waters in which they have an interest. However, all collaborative agreements, the report insists, must recognize existing intellectual property rights of the indigenous people and establish royalty payments in line with relevant international standards. The use of biological knowledge in scientific, commercial and public domains should only proceed with the approval of the traditional owners of that knowledge and the further 'collection' of such knowledge should deliver social and economic benefits to the knowledge owners. Recognizing that Aboriginal and Torres Strait Islander communities have an interest in the preservation of endangered and vulnerable species, the *Strategy* also recommends cooperative strategies aimed at species recovery and habitat preservation, especially on Aboriginal lands. At the same time it acknowledges that traditional harvesting of wildlife is important to both the cultural heritage and economy of indigenous communities and consequently it supports the continuation of such harvesting practices. To safeguard the rights of indigenous communities, the *Strategy* recommends that all arrangements aimed at fulfilling Australia's obligations under the Convention on Biological Diversity should also take into account the protocols developed by the United Nations Commission on Human Rights.

However, in practice, promising ethnobiological programmes have not been able to sustain government support. For example, the Northern Territory government has radically reduced funding to the very productive ethnobiology programme of the Northern Territory Parks and Wildlife Commission in a region where the encyclopaedic wealth of the extant indigenous languages and knowledge systems is in danger of being lost as aboriginal peoples are increasingly pressured to assimilate into the white settler society. Since the publication of the *National Strategy* there has been no progress made toward achieving its recommendations that specifically concern Aboriginal and Torres Strait Islander peoples. The proposed new approaches to collaborative conservation programmes with indigenous peoples have been undermined by Australian governments that increasingly favour sectoral interests over the interests of indigenous communities to the extent that the rights of indigenous people have been further reduced by statutory regulation.

RECONCEPTUALIZING INDIGENOUS RELATIONSHIPS WITH THE NATURAL WORLD

The rubric of Western discourses of conservation can be misleading in examining indigenous capacity to respond to resource-use challenges. Basic terms in the conservation literature require some reconceptualizing in order to address the issues for Aboriginal engagement with sustainable management of wildlife, including commercial use of wildlife. For instance, the term 'conservation' cannot be used in a presumed common-sense way without bringing within the ambit of the term some of the cultural differences often overlooked in the conservation literature. A typical example of the absence of the human dimensions in consideration of resource-use problems is the social and, often, statutory privilege granted to environmental impact assessment over social impact assessments. The pre-eminence given to scientifically adduced environmental questions over human issues is, unfortunately, unremarkable in the indigenous world, where human populations are regularly relocated and lifeways disrupted by major projects, such as dams, mines, roads, and pipelines.

Western conservationists are increasingly aware of the dilemmas for indigenous peoples, and yet considerations of equity and justice remain peripheral in the delivery of national and regional conservation programmes and resources. For example, the attention that conservation organizations devote within developing nations to the protection of non-human biota, including pets, is staggering when compared to the level of understanding displayed towards small hunter-gatherer populations. Conservation—as a general descriptor of human activities that are intended to mitigate against environmental degradation and biodiversity loss—refers primarily to human decision-making about wise use of resources and maintenance of the natural and cultural values of land, water and biota. How humans make decisions, however, is dependent on their cultural, social, political and economic contexts. Aboriginal decision-making styles are of relevance to the development and design of conservation policy and planning, yet this is rarely acknowledged in the conservation literature.

Furthermore, such literature ignores even more fundamental questions—such as how a resource is defined by different resource users and owners. A typical example of a cultural assumption in conservation thinking, especially in the science disciplines, is that a resource is defined simply as a physical commodity without regard to its human values and significance.

It was only in the 1980s and 1990s in Australia that the biota and human and technological resources have been studied, surveyed and understood as a result of regional studies by research bodies.[4] The ongoing accretion of scientific literature and data collection by a myriad of government agencies, statutory authorities, research institutions and universities has extended our knowledge of these issues. Researchers from a range of disciplines concerned with the natural world were attracted to the regions where high biodiversity values remain. However, the coincidence of these research areas with the indigenous domain was not a significant factor in the research design. As a result, much of the data was of little use to indigenous conservation managers, nor was it intended to help them. The value of the data for indigenous people has been further reduced by the apparent unwillingness of relevant bodies to return the information to indigenous land-owners in a form that can be accessed by people with low levels of Western education. It is not accidental that conservation policy and research which has been most useful to indigenous landowners has usually been commissioned by indigenous representative bodies, such as local councils, land councils and regional resource management groups. This reflects the differing priorities and economic, social and cultural frameworks employed by indigenous and non-indigenous interests.

As a subject for human decision-making, conservation cannot be deemed a discrete field because of the relevance of social, cultural, economic and political factors that must be taken into account by any group of decision-makers. In short, the problem is not one of conservation alone, or one of conservation versus development. There is a much more complex mix of conservation *and* subsistence and development issues. Furthermore, decision-making takes place in a range of situations. 'Traditional' institutions of indigenous societies—such as customary kin-based corporations—and indigenous jurisdictions provide just one context for

---

[4] Examples of such research include the reports of the Cape York Peninsula Land Use Strategy (see Cape York Regional Advisory Group 1996), the Co-operative Research Centre for the Sustainable Development of Tropical Savannas (see Co-operative Research Centre for the Sustainable Use of Tropical Savannas April 1996), Wet Tropics Management Authority (see Wet Tropics Management Authority 1992), the Great Barrier Reef Marine Park Authority (see Bergin 1993), and, as well, the studies and inquiries conducted by the Resource Assessment Commission (see Resource Assessment Commission, Coastal Zone Inquiry 1993), and the Australian Heritage Commission (see for instance, Smyth 1993; Sutherland 1996, Department of Communications and the Arts 1997).

decision-making. There are also indigenous organizations—such as community councils, socio-territorial associations, land councils, statutory bodies and other administrative and representative bodies—that constitute another significant context of decision-making. Such a diversity of institutional contexts demands an analytical approach that focuses on the overall goal of enhancing indigenous participation in conservation.

Other basic concepts in the conservation literature require special discussion to explain their use and relevance in explaining indigenous involvement in conservation activities. Key words in Aboriginal conservation and management include: 'Traditional or indigenous knowledge systems', 'intellectual and cultural property', 'customary law', 'native title' and 'traditional resource rights'. These ought to be more widely understood among the community of scientists and planners involved in indigenous wildlife management projects.

The point is well made by Dews *et al.* (1997): '[It] is important to keep in mind that indigenous peoples and conservation organizations have overlapping interests, but their perceptions of what is at stake in managing resources for the future may be quite different.'

These authors identify the conflicting values between indigenous peoples and conservationists with which environmental researchers must contend (ibid.: 48):

Conservation biologists commonly operate from ideological stances which view nature as being significant apart from human involvement while indigenous groups do not separate the two. Indigenous peoples must provision themselves from the natural environment, whereas conservation agencies are interested in protecting vanishing wilderness areas from human predation and excessive exploitation.

Issues of scale—especially in conservation planning and programme delivery for small-scale societies with traditional, as opposed to post-industrial, relations to land—assume a special significance. As Dews *et al.* note, indigenous groups tend to operate from a local perspective whereas conservation biologists and planners are concerned with large-scale, regional, if not hemispheric or global processes, and believe they are acting in behalf of the planet as a whole. It is often the case, however, that the claims by conservationists to global outcomes are grossly overstated. Even the Convention on Trade in Endangered Species (CITES) and the Convention on Biological Diversity (CBD), which are global agreements among countries, rely on implementation within countries for their effectiveness. The CITES public material explains that effective conservation actions generally take place nationally and locally and not at the global level. There are very few mechanisms to conserve species above the national level.

Most indigenous groups who are resident on their traditional territories
are small-scale; indigenous societies have been classified in the sociological
literature as small-scale on the basis, not just of their population size, but
of the types of institutions and decision-making styles which are typical in
these societies. It is important, however, to emphasize that while traditional ecological knowledge is undeniably local, and specific to place and
people (Rose 1996: 32), it is nevertheless the case that some responses of
indigenous groups to global pressures show that innovative, small-scale
commercial valuation and monitoring of wildlife—which rely on indigenous knowledge—can lead to sustainable management of species endemic
to regions with even wider migration patterns. Such responses can deliver
modes of practice that are far better than the 'solutions' advocated by
remote and standardized national systems.

In Australian Aboriginal societies there is an established body of indigenous laws that allocates rights and interests of particular people to features
of the natural world. Aboriginal property relations are 'a sacred endowment'. They derive from the sacred ancestral past that imbues the present,
shaping and forming the world we inhabit with its distinctive features and,
notably, placing individual and group entities and polities in jural relationships with attendant rights and responsibilities, according to religious
principles. These property relations are then expressed metaphorically in
the Aboriginal discourse of possession and stewardship, symbolized in a
variety of ways, particularly as iconic or totemic relationships with the
species and features of the natural world.

Such ways of conceptualizing the world have been referred to through-
out the indigenous literature that has emerged in the last few decades. For
example, a conference held in Vancouver in February 2000, 'Protecting
Knowledge: Traditional Resource Rights in the New Millennium'[5] issued
The Spirit of the Conference Statement, which stated in part: 'Indigenous
Peoples' heritage is not a commodity, nor the property of the nation-state.
The material and intellectual heritage of each Indigenous People is a sacred
gift and a responsibility that must be honoured and held for the benefit of
future generations.'

Similarly, the foundation of Australian Aboriginal biogeography
approaches this engagement with the non-human world through the lens
of the *a priori* sacred landscape peopled by spiritual Beings and imbued
with the essence of both human and non-human beings. The appropriation
of a landscape full of danger and serendipity by the geomantic reading of
places imbued with spiritual meaning inscribes the landscape with the laws

    [5] 'Protecting Knowledge: Traditional Resource Rights in the New Millennium', Spirit of
the Conference Statement. Vancouver: University of British Columbia, First Nations
House of Learning, 24–26 February 2000.

of ritual engagement with ancestors and spiritual Beings. This is a process overseen by a hierarchy of Elders who have acquired the ritual knowledge and a system of property relations from those ancestors. The ancestral legacy is both the nature of our being and the nature of our relationship to places in the landscape.

Anthropologist Nancy Williams (1998: 4–5) describes 'the relationship of Aboriginal Australians to their environment' as arising from 'the religious basis of their proprietary interests in land and the plants and animals that are a part of that environment'. From three decades of study of Yolngu people she concludes that:

This relationship is expressed *inter alia* in terms that have been labeled 'traditional ecological knowledge.' Within that body of knowledge are embedded the principles and prescriptions for the management of the environment as well as their moral basis. Aboriginal people regard the environment as sentient and as communicating with them.

Jean Christie (1996: 65) refers to the intellectual integrity of indigenous peoples:

For indigenous peoples, their lands and waters underpin who they are and are the foundation of their very survival as peoples. Over and over again, when reflecting on biodiversity or indigenous knowledge, indigenous people from all over the globe insist that living things cannot be separated from the land they grow on, and that peoples' knowledge and myriad uses of natural resources cannot be separated from their culture, and their survival as peoples on the land. This oneness—of land and the things that live in it, of people, their knowledge and their cultural connection with the land—is the only basis for meaningful consideration of biodiversity and indigenous knowledge about it. What is at stake is the intellectual integrity of peoples, not simply intellectual property.

In his study of central Australian Aboriginal people's perceptions of land management issues Bruce Rose (1995: ix) found that:

Aboriginal people see caring for country as an integral part of living on their land. Caring for country forms part of the relationship individuals have with each other and with the land. It is not seen as a separate activity which must be 'carried out'. From this perspective the most important issues are land ownership and access to land so that Aboriginal people can care for their country.

When he questioned these people about 'European notions of conservation', Rose (ibid., xvii) found that:

Aboriginal 'management' of the environment is understood through song and ceremony. It is seen to be more of an integrated process whereby knowledge of the natural world is gathered through personal experience and passed on through tradition and culture. Aboriginal management links people to their environment rather than giving them dominion over it. Aboriginal relationships to land are defined in terms of culture and site protection, land usage and harvesting of natural resources.

Extant indigenous cultures in Australia regard land not just as a physical resource, but as a social resource—as customary estates or landscapes shaped by *a priori* spiritual forces and imbued with spiritual power. Indigenous laws acknowledge that the world around us is constructed spiritually, socially and jurally. In Australian Aboriginal land tenure systems, the basic nature of property as a thing is that it is transmissible across generations—i.e., that it is a bequest or an endowment, and that the temporal dimension of endowment implies legitimacy derived from the authority of the past. The temporal dimension imbues an instance of property—an owned place—with a meaning beyond its fate of being already there: its meaning is social and institutionalized, and above all rule-governed, or subject to law. The transmission of rights in a thing across generations involves applications of law relating to the nature of a bequest that is acceded to by other members of a society or group. The regulation of matters, such as who may inherit the property and under what conditions, constitutes law when it is acceded to as tradition and custom among members of a group.

Under Aboriginal law, permission to enter another person's territory and to use the resources of that place must be sought from the appropriate traditional owners. Upon granting their consent, these owners would perform particular rituals to ensure the spiritual safety of their guests during their visit to the estate. Entry to an Aboriginal estate, and access to its resources, are subject to Aboriginal laws. As Williams has further observed, in north-eastern Arnhem Land, Yolngu land-owning groups organize responsibility for management of their estates through a set of checks and balances expressed through links of kinship. A patrilineal group (a clan) holds title to an estate, but that group cannot unilaterally make decisions on important matters concerning the estate, whether the issue is deemed to be—in non-Aboriginal terms—religious or economic. Not only must individuals related through women to the land-owning group be consulted, they must concur in the decision. Within the title-holding group, authority determined by age prevails in decision-making related to the land of that group. The authority of elders, as knowledgeable persons capable of ensuring spiritual safety, is a fundamental feature of indigenous life. Such elders are not merely senior in age, although that is often the case. Such persons, by virtue of their knowledge and, typically, ritual status, hold jural positions based on a range of personal, organizational and structural factors. These would include seniority in a particular kin-based group, religious responsibilities acquired through attention to ceremonial duties, and authority in matters of land tenure and local political and economic issues which affect the affairs of the group.

The primary ethic expressed in indigenous relationships with the natural world is that of the responsibility of stewardship for the non-human species and habitats, with these responsibilities having the force of jural principles. These jural principles are expressed, for instance, in the so-called 'totemic' affiliations established by the ancestral beings whose adventures are recorded in religious mythology. Aboriginal beliefs about the place of humans in the natural world construct a different concept of personal identity from that which is conventionally understood in Western epistemology. The Aboriginal person—as the socialized cultural being—is conceived of as not merely a body enclosing a singular conscious being. Rather, the person is conceived of as spatialized by virtue of totemic affiliations. Persons with inherited spiritual essence in common with non-human beings share the world of those beings—including their natural habitats—as a personal responsibility.

Aboriginal people hold, therefore, that the possibility of the extinction of a species, whether fauna or flora, or the destruction of what is called 'biodiversity' in environment-speak, is offensive to the nature of human existence. Aboriginal resistance to attempts to suppress their involvement with the natural world, by continuing to use fire according to tradition, for example, or by organizing with experts to sustain biodiversity through weed control, are expressions of these cultural values. They sit alongside, and interrogate, the initiatives taken to ensure the viability of Aboriginal culture through incorporation into the global economy and related developments, such as the spread of technological infrastructure. The maintenance of Aboriginal culture, particularly social relationships with land conceived of in a supra-kinship discourse, is held in Aboriginal law to be fundamental to the well-being of human society and non-human society alike—the former bearing a special responsibility for wise and respectful use of the latter.

The Aboriginal cosmology poses a different set of relational values between human and non-human from the hierarchy of values attributed to biota, landscape features and other subjects of Western natural science, and the application of those values under the rubric of 'natural and cultural values'. In practical applications, such as in the privileging of environmental over social impact assessment, this Western hierarchy assumes that Aboriginal traditional relationships with the non-human environment are irrelevant to the capacity of fauna and flora populations to reproduce themselves. Biological research concerning early human populations and fire in tropical northern Australian regions in recent times shows that this assumption must be reconsidered for the traditional Aboriginal domain.

This is not to deny that the Aboriginal domain is changing because of population growth; increasing Aboriginal participation in the economy of rural Australia, changes in the biophysical environment, and changes in the political, social and legal climate. Nevertheless, the influence of Aboriginal customs and law remain significant, and this has global implications for conservation of biodiversity. The activities of Aboriginal land managers demonstrate that a materialist consideration is necessary to an understanding of human–nature relations in the indigenous domain; and those relations are necessarily, economic, and have been so since the evolution of the human species. If we admit that Aboriginal people are fully sentient and intellectual beings, we can admit that they would engage with the effects of the global economy and information society, and that they would bring to these problems interesting and innovative approaches.

INDIGENOUS RESPONSES TO THE PRESSURES OF DEVELOPMENT

The pressures for the development of the remote areas in which the indigenous domain is largely located are a persistent and dominant feature of national political life. The key industries in rural and remote Australia are mining, pastoralism and tourism—all land-based. Because of the primacy of these industries in the rural economy, the models of economic development presently available to indigenous communities include radical alteration at various scales of the land and waters and the importation of conventional European management systems and expertise. This occurs also in protected areas because all national parks are subject to management plans, many of which marginalize indigenous land use and management.

In the context of their limited ability to resist incorporation into the global economy, increasing reliance on western technology and infrastructure—and facing a population explosion and increasing poverty and disadvantage—the challenge for indigenous groups is to develop economic niches to sustain their ways of life and to sustainably manage their environments. For Aboriginal groups considering their futures, wildlife harvesting is regarded as a high priority for further development because they already have the necessary skills and knowledge which flow, ironically, from a localized way of life. There are a number of indigenous enterprises that utilize wildlife. These include: crocodile egg harvesting for sale to hatcheries with royalty payments to traditional owners; harvesting of seed for regeneration of mine sites; harvesting of marine life such as fish pearl shell, trochus and crayfish; supply of 'bush tucker' and bush condiments to the restaurant trade; the use of subsistence hunting by-products (feathers, bone, etc.) in craft products; the production of artifacts and art from bush materials; the harvesting of didgeridoo sticks; the semi-domestication of native honey-bag bees; trepang harvesting and processing; the harvesting and production of bush medicines and the propagation of trees and shrubs for regeneration and landscaping. Because industries based on wildlife harvesting enable indigenous people to use their existing knowledge and skills they offer opportunities for small-scale enterprises that create small but useful levels of income. Where the operation of these enterprises is a natural adjunct to life in their homelands the levels of benefits derived could be significant given the marginal effort required.

Small-scale commercial use of natural resources presents options for developing Aboriginal approaches to the sustainable stewardship of their traditional land and water estates. The benefits include the development of appropriate levels of economic development under the control of traditional hunting and gathering groups whose ways of life are jeopardized by sedentarism. These economic activities are a suitable accompaniment to the practices of traditional hunting and gathering, and, importantly, they do not create cultural conflicts over potential breaches of Aboriginal law concerning totemic affiliation with the particular species. Appropriate senior clan members must authorize access to estates and any activities carried out on them, including traditional hunting and gathering *and* commercial harvesting of native and non-native species. Small-scale ventures are compatible with traditional law and culture because compliance is possible at this scale and non-compliance can be redressed according to tradition.

So far initiatives taken in this area have been based, in part, on the notion that commercial valuation of wildlife constitutes a fundamental protective measure for sustaining populations of species under threat from human impacts. The valuation itself accords the species a status as a potentially non-renewable resource that must be managed sustainably. For example, in central Arnhem Land in the Northern Territory of Australia, an Aboriginal land management scheme operated by an association of traditional land owners, Bawinanga, operates a crocodile (*Crocodylus porosus*) egg harvesting venture. In the 1980s, commercial crocodile farms sought permission from the Northern Territory Government to harvest crocodile eggs on Aboriginal land. The Yolngu response was to commence harvesting arrangements of their own to prevent the opening up of the resource to non-Aboriginal operators who might have been given the opportunity to exploit the resource unsustainably (*Crocodylus porosus* was almost hunted to extinction by commercial white hunters before bans were introduced in early 1971). Since 1990 local rangers have gathered crocodile eggs from a number of central Arnhem Land river systems. The eggs are hatched and transported to a specialist agency in Darwin for sale to domestic and international markets.

The harvesting is monitored by experts and Aboriginal staff. Following the recovery of the crocodile population after their protection in 1971, over 100,000 eggs and 6,000 animals have been harvested in the Northern Territory by commercial operators up until 1994. It is not easy to monitor the impacts of such harvesting, but there is every reason to expect the harvest to be sustainable. However, in 1997 senior elders of the local Yolngu clans rejected a proposal for a trial harvest of adult saltwater crocodiles for the skin trade and local subsistence use of meat, reasoning that commercial harvesting of adults ran counter to the great respect accorded in customary beliefs to these creatures. The religious observance of the ancestral crocodile totemic being in ceremonial life is regionally important, uniting all human descendants and their reptilian cohorts in common interest.

The application of local indigenous laws and the concern of local traditional owners for high biodiversity values are critical to sustaining highly localized species populations in the indigenous domain. Dean Yibarbuk, Gongorni leader from the Bawinanga association, makes this point about the impact of poorly managed fire in his homelands:

Today fire is not being well looked after. Some people, especially younger people who don't know better or who don't care, sometimes just chuck matches anywhere without thinking of the law and culture of respect that we have for fire. This is especially true for people just going for weekends away from the big settlement. Fire is being managed well around the outstations where people live all the time.

It was Yibarbuk's attention to such environmental details that alerted environmental scientists to the problem of wildfires in the regions which had been vacated by Aboriginal people under the Australian government's assimilation programme of the 1950s. Yibarbuk and other men of the central Arnhem Land region have addressed this problem by taking traditional people to these areas and replicating, with some caution, the burning regimes that once protected the region from hot wildfires. They have obtained the cooperation and assistance of a number of agencies in their efforts.

As mentioned, Aboriginal communities are attracted to small-scale harvesting ventures because they are amenable to the traditional forms of governance and, increasingly, throughout Arnhem Land and central Australia, such communities have collaborated with research bodies to undertake monitoring in order to guide their decisions regarding the sustainable harvesting of specific species and protection of their habitats. There is, of course, an ancient tradition of wildlife trading within and between the indigenous nations in Australia and with our near Asian neighbours. Now it offers new opportunities for the development of sustainable industries that are accessible to indigenous people. There is scope to develop industries that are appropriate in scale and in capital and technical requirements and which are conducive to traditional practices regarding the management of natural and cultural environments.

RECOGNITION OF TRADITIONAL RESOURCE RIGHTS AND SUSTAINABLE PRACTICES

The recognition of traditional resource rights, benefit-sharing, control of access and intellectual property, and the development of mechanisms to facilitate the commercial involvement of indigenous people in resource exploitation are important for the success of indigenous people's life in their homelands. However, there is a different starting-point in terms of the resource rights of indigenous peoples in the jurisdictions of different settler states throughout the world. There is wide variation in both the rights of indigenous people and the extent to which they are able to enjoy those rights. As the UN Special Rapporteur Madame Daes pointed out in a 1999 Report to the Human Rights Commission, most countries where indigenous people live assert a power to extinguish the rights of those people 'most often without just compensation'. The doctrine of extinguishment, Madame Daes noted, is something that 'came into prominent use during the colonial period'.

Australia is unique among the former British colonies in that no recognized treaty was ever concluded with any indigenous group. The indigenous peoples in Australia are in a comparable situation to the native peoples of South America and Asia where there is a low standard of domestic recognition of civil and political rights, and indeed, high levels of breaching human rights in general. Under the doctrine of *terra nullius*, Aboriginal traditional resource rights were believed to be wiped away by Crown sovereignty. Even though some limited legal recognition of indigenous rights has emerged in the last twenty-five years, this has coincided with the advance of market forces into the indigenous domain. In recent years these limited rights have been eroded by a resurgent white nationalist agenda pursued by the federal government and some of the states.

Traditional resource rights in Australia have been procured in two ways: by statutory recognition of rights under the 'grace and favour of the Crown' or by case law. Statutory recognition of resource rights has concerned, in the main, access rights to special forms of title over Aboriginal land for mineral, gas and oil exploration and extraction. Case law—following the Mabo No. 2 decision of the High Court of Australia—has found, for limited areas, Aboriginal customary rights and entitlements in resources, including water. In the Mabo No. 2 case, the judges found that native title—i.e. the land tenure system that pre-existed the arrival of British law—had survived the annexation of Australia to the Crown under particular circumstances, and that it could be recognized at common law. However, they also confirmed the power of the sovereign to extinguish native title.

Two recent cases have particular significance. First, in supporting a native title claim by the Miriuwung and Gajerrong people in Western Australia, the Federal Court ruled that they had the right to 'possess, occupy, use and enjoy' the land that they claimed and either use it as they saw fit or 'receive a portion of any resources taken by others'. Of particular significance is the fact that the judgement included the allocation and use of water rights and it could lay the ground for a new configuration of jural, economic and social relationships between the indigenous and settler societies. Secondly, the High Court recently upheld the right of Aboriginal activist Marandoo Yanner to hunt for crocodiles in the area his people come from after he had initially been charged with killing a protected species under the Queensland Fauna Act. Yanner had succeeded in having the charges against him dismissed in a Magistrate's Court before the Magistrate's decision was overturned on appeal. In a majority decision, the judges of the High Court found that the magistrate had been right in ruling that the Fauna Act 'did not prohibit or restrict the appellant, as a native title holder, from hunting or fishing for the crocodiles he took for the purpose of satisfying personal, domestic or non-commercial communal needs'. Although this ruling imposes limits on Aboriginal resource rights (i.e., for non-commercial use only), it was a breakthrough in the recognition of Aboriginal rights in Australia.

In the United States, by contrast, treaty rights have given the indigenous people stronger legal protection as long as the courts have been willing to support the intention of the treaties. Treaties between governments and Indian peoples included the premise that water—like trees, grass and air— was integral to the concept of land dealt with under such treaties. Over the years, increasing development pressures have encouraged a variety of forces to seek to separate land and water rights, yet a number of significant decisions have resisted this separation. This is especially the case in relation to fishing rights (Levy 1998).

Indian rights to water in the US are also supported by the Winter's decision of 1908, which ruled that the doctrine of 'prior use' applied to the use of water. Sixty years after this decision the Umatilla Confederated Tribes in Oregon were able to cite the Winter's doctrine in a successful 1977 suit, in which they argued that the Army Corps of Engineers, in constructing the Chief Joseph Dam, had illegally interfered with the water flow necessary for the spawning of salmon and steelhead trout that were the basis of the Umatilla people's economy.

At the same time case law in the United States has also resulted in the extinguishment or impairment of Indian rights. For example, in the case of the Tee-Hit-Ton Indians v. United States, the US Supreme Court extinguished the rights of the Tee-Hit-Ton people without compensation, even though the US Constitution explicitly states that the government may not take property without due process of law and just compensation (Daes 1999). The legal doctrine created by this case has been widely invoked and, indeed, Congress relied on it in 1971 when it voted to extinguish the land claims of nearly all of the 226 nations and tribes of Alaska under the Alaska Native Claims Settlement Act. This act transferred some of the land to profit-making corporations that the indigenous people were required to set up so that these same corporations could then sell the land at much less than the market value. The tribes themselves were paid no money at all and the land that was not claimed by indigenous corporations was turned over to the state of Alaska or the federal government. Needless to say, the Alaskan tribes did not consent to this legislation.

In 1978 the Canadian Inupiat leader Eben Hopson (1978) said:

If we are to enjoy our Inuit hunting rights we must also be able to manage our land. With great care taken, our land can yield its subsurface wealth to the world, but we Inuit have the right to determine just how much care must be taken. Proceeding from our native hunting rights is the right to manage and protect our subsistence game habitat safe from harm. Our subsistence hunting rights must be the core of any successful Arctic resource management regime.

This followed the settlement of a pioneering land claim in the James Bay Northern Quebec Agreement. This agreement has been followed by two other important land claim agreements affecting the Arctic region: the Inuvialuit Final Agreement and the Nunavut Land Claims Agreement. These three agreements establish constitutionally protected access to resources. They establish rights, titles and interests in land and provide various degrees of land ownership, including access by non-beneficiaries. Surface and subsurface rights are detailed as well as the establishment of co-management bodies with varying degrees of responsibility and funding for research and resource use planning. The agreements allow for monetary compensation and environmental and social impact assessment processes. There is no ownership of wildlife under the agreements but rather varying degrees of constitutionally protected priority access. All three of the land claim agreements mentioned above list conservation as a core principle of community-based resource management.

While some national jurisdictions may offer limited protection of indigenous resource rights acknowledged under treaties, case law, or statutes, it is the international jurisdiction that constructs the regulatory space in which trade in wildlife is limited. CITES—the Convention on International Trade in Endangered Species of Wild Fauna and Flora—has been in effect since 1975, and the capacity of indigenous peoples to comply with the Convention has so far been proven to be at least as good as that of ratifying nation-states. Specifically, CITES protects threatened species from all international commercial trade, regulates trade in species not threatened with extinction but which may become threatened if trade goes unregulated, and gives countries the option of listing native species that are already protected within their own borders. The Convention embraces the view that trade in protected plant and animal species can be carried out on a sustainable basis and its effectiveness is regularly reviewed at conferences and other forums where amendments can be proposed and adopted. CITES conferences allow for attendance of non-voting non-governmental organizations representing conservation, animal welfare, trade, zoological, and scientific interests and they frequently discuss traditional resource rights in the context of other political agendas. Indigenous spokespeople are generally marginalized by the aggressive and well-resourced delegations representing the member states and large international organizations.

The 'regulatory space' constructed by CITES and other international convention monitoring bodies has impacted on the indigenous world both beneficially and detrimentally. Traditional resource rights of indigenous peoples may be discussed more often, however, it is in the hegemonic discourses of such international bodies that local traditional and indigenous discourses become ensnared when global interests—whether corporate or regulatory—oppose the local populations and claim a regulatory authority over them. International law of previous centuries, which authorized or justified the colonization of indigenous peoples, constituted a hegemonic discourse with profound impacts. The powerful members of CITES are the very same nation-states which systematically discriminated against the encapsulated indigenous populations and they continue to appropriate indigenous property according to remnant imperial doctrines still held at law.

CONCLUSION

Sustainable use of biodiversity in remnant indigenous homelands provides both opportunities for the maintenance of indigenous cultures and ways of life and, at the same time, for the development of an enduring indigenous economic base that would reduce social and economic inequity typical of most indigenous populations. Yet, for many indigenous peoples, the options for economic pathways to sustainability of ancient ways of life are hampered by the restriction of their harvesting rights to customary rights by both national and international regulation.

As we have seen, customary hunting and gathering is a contentious issue, and one can expect from the present antagonism to indigenous use of natural resources that indigenous commercial use of natural products might be even more contentious.

In these circumstances, the framework for developing *sui generis* options for protection and compensation for indigenous peoples from traditional resource use, as proposed by Posey and Duttfield (1996), has a special significance in the absence of protection of these rights by any Convention and the vulnerability of such rights in domestic jurisdictions.

The injustice that this situation involves for indigenous peoples is, as I have explained here, not just a continuation of the long and terrible history of imperial dominion. There is more at stake in general than the impoverishment and dispossession of local small-scale societies, such as hunting and gathering peoples. The issue is one of a steadily advancing environmental crisis. Along with the potential or actual environmental degradation, the slowness of the advances—where there are any at all—in the recognition of the contribution of indigenous peoples to the maintenance of biological diversity may contribute to the collapse of faunal and floral species that have been maintained by these groups for much of human history. Arguments and the accretion of evidence as to the contribution that indigenous peoples might make to sustaining biodiversity through cautious commercial harvesting in their local areas where the global market persistently encroaches thus become more urgent.

This survey of the vexed web of issues relating to sustainable environments in indigenous domains shows just how fragile the resource rights of indigenous peoples are, and this fragility itself emerges as a factor of great significance in the problem of thinking about indigenous futures. Hence, the issue of indigenous proprietary interests in the features of the natural world poses the potential for strategies for successful indigenous management of natural resources. If such proprietary interests were interpreted more widely than the fossilized postcolonial view of native peoples as having mere customary subsistence rights, the opportunities for rigorous assessment of non-subsistence harvesting might be elaborated beyond the rare instances we find at present.

REFERENCES

Australia ICOMOS (International Council on Monuments and Sites) (1997). *The Burra Charter: the Australia ICOMOS Charter on Caring for Places of Cultural Significance* (revised version). Kingston, ACT: ICOMOS.

Bergin, A. (1993). *Aboriginal and Torres Strait Islander Interests in the Great Barrier Reef Marine Park*, Townsville, Queensland: Great Barrier Reef Marine Park Authority (Research Publication No. 31).

Bomford, M. and J. Caughley (eds.) (1996). *Sustainable Use of Wildlife by Aboriginal Peoples and Torres Strait Islanders.* Canberra: Bureau of Resource Sciences, Australian Government Publishing Service.

Cape York Regional Advisory Group (1996). CYPLUS Draft Stage 2: *A Strategy for Sustainable Land Use and Economic and Social Development.* Cairns: Department of Local Government and Planning, and Canberra: Department of the Environment, Sport and Territories.

Christie, J. (1996). 'Biodiversity and intellectual property rights: implications for indigenous peoples', in Sultan *et al., Ecopolitics IX Conference: Perspectives on Indigenous Peoples' Management of the Environmental Resources: Darwin, 1995.* Darwin: Northern Land Council.

Co-operative Research Centre for the Sustainable Use of Tropical Savannas (April 1996). Draft Strategic Plan, NT.

Daes, E. A. (Special Rapporteur) (1999). *Human Rights of Indigenous Peoples: Indigenous People and their Relationship to Land,* Second progress report on the working paper. Commission on Human Rights, Sub-Commission on Prevention of Discrimination and Protection of Minorities, /CN.4/Sub.2/1999/183, June 1999.

Department of Communications and the Arts (1997). *Heritage Places: Past, Present and Future* (Draft Guidelines for the Protection, Management and Use of Aboriginal and Torres Strait Islander Cultural Heritage Places). Canberra: Department of Communications and the Arts.

Dews, G., J. David, J. Cordell, F. Ponte and Torres Strait Island Co-ordinating Council (1997). *Indigenous Protected Area Feasibility Study.* Report prepared for Environment Australia and the Torres Strait Island Co-ordinating Council. Unpublished.

Dobkin de Rios, Marlene (1992). *Amazon Healer: The Life and Time of an Urban Shaman.* Bridport: Prism.

Furze, B., T. De Lacy and J. Birckhead (1996). *Culture, Conservation, and Biodiversity: The Social Dimension of Linking Local Level Development and Conservation through Protected Areas,* Chichester: John Wiley.

Goodman, D. (1996). 'Land claim agreements and the management of whaling in the Canadian Arctic', *Proceedings 11th International Symposium on Peoples and Cultures of the North*. Abashiri: Hokkaido Museum of Northern Peoples. URL: http://www.highnorth.no/Library/Policies/National/la-cl-ag.htm

Gray, A. (1997). *The Explosion of Aboriginality: Components of Indigenous Population Growth 1991–96*, Discussion Paper No. 142, Centre for Aboriginal Economic Policy Research. Canberra: Australian National University.

Hopson, E. (1978). *Hopson's Address to the London Press Corps 23 June*. URL: http://www.buchholdt.com/EbenHopson/papers/1978/London.html

Janke, T. (1997). *Our Culture, Our Future: Proposals for Recognition and Protection of Indigenous Cultural and Intellectual Property*. Canberra: Australian Institute of Aboriginal and Torres Strait Islander Studies, Aboriginal and Torres Strait Islander Commission. URL: http://www.icip.lawnet.com.au

Kohen, J. (1995). *Aboriginal Environmental Impacts*. Sydney: University of New South Wales Press, .

Levy, R. (1998). Appendix to *Native Title Offshore — Exclusive Possession or Coexistence?* Unpublished.

National Strategy for the Conservation of Australia's Biological Diversity (1996). Canberra: Department of the Environment, Sport and Territories.

Nietschmann, B. Q. (1992). *The Interdependence of Biological and Cultural Diversity*. Kenmore, WA: Centre for World Indigenous Studies, Occasional Paper 21.

Posey, D. A. (1996). *Traditional Resource Rights. International Instruments for Protection and Compensation for Indigenous Peoples and Local Communities*. Gland, Switzerland, and Cambridge, UK: IUCN.

Posey, D. A. and G. Dutfield (1996). *Beyond Intellectual Property: Toward Traditional Resource. Rights for Indigenous Peoples and Local Communities*, Ottawa: International Development Research Centre.

Resource Assessment Commission, (1993). *Coastal Zone Inquiry, Final Report*. Canberra: Resource Assessment Commission.

Rose, B. (1995). *Land Management Issues: Attitudes and Perceptions amongst Aboriginal People of Central Australia*. Alice Springs: CLC.

Rose, D. B. (1996). *Nourishing Terrains. Australian Aboriginal Views of Landscape and Wilderness*. Canberra: Australian Heritage Commission.

Smyth, D. (1993). *A Voice in All Places: Aboriginal and Torres Strait*

Islander Interests in Australia's Coastal Zone. Consultancy Report, Resource Assessment Commission, revised edn. Canberra: Coastal Zone Inquiry.

Spinks, P. (1999). *Wizards of Oz : Recent Breakthroughs by Australian Scientists.* St Leonards, NSW: Allen & Unwin.

Spirit of the Conference Statement, 'Protecting Knowledge: Traditional Resource Rights in the New Millennium'. Vancouver: University of British Columbia, First Nations House of Learning, 24–26 February 2000.

Stevens, S. and T. De Lacey (eds.) (1997). *Conservation through Cultural Survival: Indigenous Peoples and Protected Areas,* Washington DC: Island Press.

Sutherland, J. (1996). *Fisheries, Aquaculture and Aboriginal and Torres Strait Islander Peoples: Studies, Policies and Legislation.* Commissioned by the Department of Environment, Sport and Territories, Canberra.

Taylor, J. (1997). *Changing Numbers, Changing Needs? A Preliminary Assessment of Indigenous Population Growth 1991–96,* Discussion Paper, No. 42. Canberra: Australian National University, Centre for Aboriginal Economic Policy Research.

Waitangi Tribunal (1999). *Whanganui River Report, 28 June 1999.* URL: http://www.knowledge-basket.co.nz/oldwaitangi/whanganui/index. htm

Wet Tropics Management Authority (1992). *Wet Tropics Plan: Strategic Directions.* Cairns.

Williams, N. (1998). *Intellectual Property and Aboriginal Environmental Knowledge.* Darwin: Centre for Indigenous Natural and Cultural Resource Management, Northern Territory University.

INDEX

Note: **emboldened** pages indicate chapters